Miss Clara Baur, founder of the Cincinnati Conservatory of Music

Miss Bertha Baur 1912

Bertha Baur:
A Woman of Note

by

Helen Board

DORRANCE & COMPANY
Philadelphia

For

Alice Baur Hodges

whose inspiration and assistance made
possible the publication of this book

CONTENTS

FOREWORD

I'll never forget my first meeting with Miss Bertha, as we called her. It was in the fall of 1928. I'd come to Cincinnati to try for a scholarship with the renowned tenor and teacher, Dan Beddoe. I had auditioned for him, and he had arranged an audition for me with Miss Baur, who made all scholarship awards.

The moment was at hand. Nervous and a bit shaky, I walked into her office. There she sat, with her beautiful white hair—handsome, regal, and with the bearing of a queen. If she'd been the Queen of England, I couldn't have been more awed. She was all business: "Young man, Mr. Beddoe has told me about you. Sing whatever you wish." Thinking that she was German and hoping to impress her, I selected Schumann's *Widmung*. After I had finished, she inquired, "What was the language? Was it Czechoslovakian?" "It was German, Miss Baur," I responded, much deflated. "Then you must come to me for diction lessons; I couldn't understand a single word."

This, I learned later, was typical of her. She was critical, businesslike, no nonsense: But she was completely dedicated to students and eager to help them. She knew students, faculty, and, as a matter of fact, everything that was going on in her school, to which she was totally dedicated.

She had a wonderful way of using words economically. I remember seeing her and a fellow student of mine pass in the corridor of old Shillito Hall. He had a high speaking voice and a tendency to drag his feet when he walked. "Young man," she siad, "lower your voice and raise your heels." She turned and was gone.

Students, faculty, staff—all of us loved her, respected her, and now that I think about it, feared her. Peter Froehlich, longtime faculty member and local wit, summed up our regard for her ability in what was then a rather risqué remark: "Miss Bertha is the smartest person alive; if she wore pants, she'd be President of the United States."

Jack M. Watson
Dean
Thomas James Kelly Professor of Music

PREFACE

When I first met Miss Bertha Baur, she was in the midst of her remarkable career as director of the Cincinnati Conservatory of Music. In the full bloom of maturity, she was gracious, confident, and assured. The youthful glow had faded, but in its place were qualities infinitely more arresting: poise, charm, and dignity. Since the death of her aunt, Miss Clara Baur, she had managed the Conservatory alone and unaided by endowment. Under her forceful, progressive leadership, the school had become internationally known, recognized for its comprehensive curriculum, its artistic standards, and the superiority of its faculty.

The Cincinnati Conservatory of Music was founded in 1867 by Miss Clara Baur, a native of Stuttgart, Germany, who had come to the United States to establish a music school along the lines of the great European conservatories of that day. Upon her aunt's death in 1912, Bertha Baur had succeeded her as director. Her name was known and respected wherever musicians congregated and wherever music was loved and performed. I recall with nostalgia the first time I saw her. The details remain in my memory as if it were yesterday.

It was a damp, misty morning in June, 1924, with overcast skies and low-hanging clouds. As I stepped from a taxicab in front of Shillito Hall, the Conservatory's main building, a stately woman with patrician features and a crown of snow white hair came out of the side entrance. She smiled and nodded as she passed near me on the driveway. A few steps farther she paused briefly and spoke to the gardener, who was working in a flower bed near the fountain. The conversation concluded, she walked briskly across the campus, seemingly oblivious to the drizzle and the wet grass. I did not know it then, but I was seeing for the first time the woman who has perhaps done more than any of her contemporaries to advance the cause of music education in the United States.

In July, 1930, Bertha Baur retired from active management of the Cincinnati Conservatory of Music, presenting the school as a gift to the city of Cincinnati through the Institute of Fine Arts. As president emeritus, she continued to occupy her residence on the campus until her death ten years later.

In 1955, the Cincinnati Conservatory of Music merged with the Cincinnati College of Music under the corporate name College-Conservatory of Music. However, because most of the events related in this volume took place long before the merger, the school is referred to as the Cincinnati Conservatory of Music or simply as "the Conservatory."

Five years after the merger, the College-Conservatory of Music became the fourteenth undergraduate college of the University of Cincinnati. In November, 1967, one hundred years after the founding of the Conservatory, the school was moved from its home in the Shillito mansion to its new location on the unversity campus, where it now occupies a magnificent complex of modern buildings, made possible by the generosity of alumni, friends, and other patrons of the arts.

For most of the material used herein, I have relied largely upon my own recollections and those of my friends and former associates, students and alumni of the school, and members of the Baur and Herzer families who were kind enough to search their records and their memories for events and episodes pertaining to the life and times of Misses Clara and Bertha Baur. I have also made use of newspaper and magazine clippings, as well as concert and recital programs found in the Conservatory scrapbooks, the only sources available, since Bertha Baur's correspondence and personal papers have been either misplaced or destroyed. Hopefully, they may yet come to light.

There were so many notable musicians who, through the years, brought distinction to the Conservatory teaching staff, that it has been difficult to decide which of these artists should be portrayed in this volume. To have mentioned each of them would have been to create an endless parade of famous names. Only those who have attained international recognition have been depicted.

I have made no attempt to write an exhaustive or comprehensive biography of Miss Bertha Baur, nor have I endeavored to enumerate her many accomplishments in the field of music education. These are too well known to require repetition. The task I set for myself was to portray this unusual woman as I knew her and worked for her during the decade in which she reached the peak of her long and distinguished career, the decade which has been called the Conservatory's "Days of Glory."

ACKNOWLEDGEMENTS

In the process of assembling the material for this volume, I was assisted by many of my friends, former co-workers at the Conservatory, alumni, and members of the Baur and Herzer families, some of whom gave access to their records, photographs, and other data concerning family relationships; others made valuable suggestions as to where additional material might be found.

Thanks are due especially to Mrs. Alice (Baur) Hodges, of Cincinnati, whose encouragement, inspiration, and gracious cooperation were indispensable in the preparation of this manuscript; to Mrs. Katherine (Baur) Lawwill, also of Cincinnati, for information on family history, vital statistics, and other memoranda; to Mrs. Virginia (Baur) Brown, of Sunland, California, for a complete copy of the *Genealogie der Familie Baur*, and to Herr Karl Baur, of Stuttgart, Germany, for his valuable research into Miss Clara Baur's early education.

I am deeply indebted to Mrs. Wanda Constance (Baur) Morse, of Pigeon, Michigan, who opened a hitherto unknown chapter in the life of Bertha Baur by giving firsthand information on the colony of *Ora Labora*, and for letters and newspaper cuttings concerning Miss Baur's father, the Reverend Emil Gottlieb Baur, who founded the colony. Through the kindness of Mrs. Morse, my understanding of Bertha Baur's childhood and adolescence has been enhanced. In this connection, I should also like to express my gratitude to Mrs. Lela Puffer, of Flint, Michigan, for allowing me to quote freely from her manuscript, *Ora Labora*.

I am most grateful to the members of the Herzer family whose help was so willingly and generously given: to Mrs. Herman A. Herzer and her daughter, Mrs. Robert C. Fawcett, of Lakewood, Ohio, who went out of their way to furnish a copy of the Herzer family genealogy and to supply information concerning their distinguished kinsman Dr. Herman Herzer, and to

Mrs. Miriam (Otto) Kockritz for her personal recollections of this famous geologist and paleontologist who was her maternal grandfather.

Among my former associates and friends at the Cincinnati Conservatory of Music, special thanks are due to Miss Flay Butler for her generous assistance with certain chapters, and for her personal recollections of Mr. George A. Baur, with whom she worked for many years in the bursar's office. I also wish to express my thanks to my former co-worker, Miss Mabel Hall, for making available certain Alumni Association scrapbooks for my use; to Mrs. Dorothy (Hull) Beatty, of Santa Barbara, California, for her vivid impressions of Miss Bertha Baur and the interesting personalities she knew during her student days at the Conservatory; to Miss Marionbelle Blocksom, former assistant dean of women, for sharing her cherished memories of the Misses Baur—Clara, Bertha, and Wanda—as well as programs and clippings which she had kept through the years, and to Dr. Marie Nast Wherry, of Cincinnati, Mrs. Mildred (Taylor) Stevens, of Macon, Georgia, and Mrs. Berenice (Jackson) Bonner, of Dallas, Texas, for certain photographs appearing in this volume.

I recall with pleasure an evening spent with Mr. H. Ray Staater, of Bluffton, Ohio and St. Petersburg, Florida, who talked entertainingly of "Miss Clara," whom he was privileged to know personally when he was a young piano teacher on her staff.

An interview with Mr. John Jacob Niles, world-famous composer and singer of folk songs who assisted the late Ralph Lyford in organizing and producing the first performances of the Cincinnati Summer Opera, was a "page from the past," both informative and nostalgic. Mrs. Lucy (de Young) Stewart and Miss Pearl Besuner, both well-known Cincinnati singers, also shared their recollections of the early days of the opera.

I found librarians to be unfailingly kind and helpful. In particular, I wish to thank Mr. Samuel F. Douglas and Mr. Donald Clawson, of the College-Conservatory of Music Library, for their friendly cooperation; Mrs. Ronald D. Shephard, curator of manuscripts of the Cincinnati Historical Society; Mrs. Margaret L. Moser, head of the history, biography and travel department of the Cleveland Public Library; Mrs. Dorothy M. McKelvey, historian of the Alumni Association of Baldwin-Wallace College, Berea, Ohio; the librarians in the Michigan Historical Collections of the University of Michigan, and the staff in the Music Room of the Cincinnati Public Library.

Many Cincinnati musicians have also graciously shared their recollections of Miss Bertha Baur and the school she guided for so many years with intelligence, wisdom, and foresight. Their help in the preparation of this volume is gratefully acknowledged although it is impossible to list all of them by name.

Chapter I

A PLACE FOR YOUTHFUL DREAMS

> If there were dreams to sell,
> What would you buy?
> Some cost a passing bell;
> Some a light sigh.
> Thomas Lovell Beddoes, *Dream-Pedlary*

Since my freshman year in high school, where amateur the-
atricals were a popular feature of the extracurricular activities, I
had been hopelessly "stage-struck." My ambition was to enroll
in the Cincinnati Conservatory of Music to prepare for a career
in musical theatre. My parents advised a more practical course
of study, realizing that my aspirations far outran my capabili-
ties. I was not convinced. By chipping away at their objections,
I finally persuaded them to allow me to enter the Conservatory
for a summer term, and agreed to earn part of my expenses.

Upon the recommendations of my voice teacher, a Conservatory graduate, and a personal friend of Miss Baur, she agreed to
accept me as a member of her secretarial staff. Sufficient time
would be given me to attend classes.

My parents were convinced that after a few weeks' hard
work and association with persons of real talent, I would realize
my limitations. They were mistaken. The splendor of great
music performed by the finest artists, the excitement of the
theatre and the enchantment of the opera only served to inspire
me to greater efforts in making the most of whatever small
talents I possessed. Miss Baur became a dear friend, a wise
counselor, and a faithful ally. I remained on her staff until the
end of the 1926-27 school term, at which time I was awarded a
diploma in dramatic art. After an interval of teaching and
further study in New York, I returned to the Conservatory to
work toward the Bachelor of Letters degree. Once again Miss
Baur welcomed me as a member of her staff, this time as her

1

personal secretary. But this is getting ahead of the story.

With high hopes and lofty aims, I set out for Cincinnati on a balmy evening in June to enter the Cincinnati Conservatory of Music. The big, northbound train glided swiftly through the soft summer night, past wooded hills, lush green pastures, and fields of freshly turned furrows. Early the next morning, after what seemed an endless night, the conductor announced that we would be in Cincinnati in thirty minutes.

We were due to arrive in the Pennsylvania Station at seven-thirty, but long before that time the tall spires of churches and the tops of skyscrapers could be seen above the morning mist. Thick folds of fog lay along the banks of the Ohio River, shrouding most of the craft riding at anchor there. The huge engine cautiously inched its way across the bridge that links Ohio with Kentucky. With a creaking and straining of gears and the harsh clanging of bells, the train eased to a stop, hissing clouds of steam in the murky light of the train shed. Clutching the large manila envelope that held my music and dramatic readings, I hurried through the vast, dim corridor and out into the mainstream of passengers. I was young, eager, and starry-eyed; not even the shower that suddenly arose was able to dampen my spirits.

On the short ride from the station, the taxicab was deftly maneuvered through the narrow, winding old streets of the "basin" area, which clearly showed the marks of an industrial city. Suddenly and unexpectedly, at the crest of a steep hill, we came upon the wide, tree-lined avenues of the suburb of Mount Auburn. Here, in contrast to the industrial area, were magnificent homes enclosed by ornate iron fences, their well-kept lawns sparkling with the recent shower. The influence of German architecture was everywhere: turrets, cupolas, ornamental carvings, and windows with stained-glass panes. A few moments more brought us to the Conservatory grounds. On either side of the entrance gates were large square posts of cut stone, and on one of the posts was a brass plaque containing the magic words: The Cincinnati Conservatory of Music. Even as we entered the grounds, an incredible volume of sound assaulted the ears: dozens of musical instruments played simultaneously in different keys and in unrelated rhythms. The effect was not unlike the tuning up of an immense symphony orchestra. Above this onslaught of dissonance, the voice students were adding an obbligato of arpeggios, scales and vocalises from which no distinct melody emerged—a musical Tower of Babel.

With its gabled windows and ferocious stone griffins guarding the entrance, the main building, Shillito Hall, imparted a fairy-tale quality. The gray limestone walls, streaked and weathered by the storms of more than half a century, looked forbidding. The heavy double doors leading into the lobby were encrusted with diamond-paned glass that glittered with jewel-like colors. When I stepped inside, my first impression was one of the vastness: vaulted ceilings, wide windows, and massive doors, reminiscent of ancient feudal castles along the Rhine. The floor of black and white marble was laid in a checkerboard pattern. To the right of the entrance was an enormous wood-burning fireplace. Above the dark walnut mantelpiece three carved figures towered to the ceiling. They represented Peace, with a dove; Harmony, holding a lyre, and Plenty, with the traditional cornucopia.[1]

Dominating the entire entrance hall and lending the only spot of color was a magnificent stained-glass window above the massive hand-carved staircase. Its vivid colors contrasted sharply with the dark paneling of the walls. The central figure was St. Cecilia in a flowing robe of crimson, seated at the organ and surrounded by allegorical figures in muted shades of green, gold, and brown.[2] Light filtering through the panes made a kaleidoscope of softly-tinted shadows on the floor beneath.

Since the hour was early and the school offices had not opened for the day, there was ample time to observe the exquisite appointments of these beautiful rooms. The spacious drawing room featured a mantel of gleaming white marble, supported on either side by carved figures depicting Winter and Summer. Suspended from the frescoed ceiling was a delicately wrought chandelier, its dozens of crystal prisms scintillating in the light. On the floor was an Oriental rug.

The library, a wood-paneled room of classical design, was directly to the left of the entrance. Over the fireplace was a large bronze tablet, and on the mantel were hand-carved masks of Dante, Shakespeare, Goethe, and other literary figures. The

Main Hall and Stairway

4

floors were made of small, intricately patterned hexagonal blocks of contrasting wood—a marvel of workmanship. The walls were lined with books, and a large mahogany table stood in the center of the room.

By nine o'clock a long line of students, waiting to be enrolled, had formed near the office door. In due time I found myself next in line and was told that Miss Baur wished to see me before I registered. A student assistant ushered me through the main office, past clicking typewriters and jangling telephones, to a small corner office with windows looking out over the side lawn. The walls of the room were literally lined with signed photographs of famous persons. Sitting at a large desk facing the door was the lady I had seen earlier that morning as she crossed the campus: the legendary Miss Bertha Baur. Even before I heard the well-modulated voice, I realized that here was an unusual woman. With a gracious smile and a firm handclasp, she made we welcome, dispelling any misgivings I may have had. She motioned me to a chair opposite her, and soon we were discussing my office duties and the course of study she wished me to pursue.

After the interview was finished, Miss Baur introduced me to the members of her staff with whom I would be working: Mrs. J. H. Benton, the registrar, a serene and gentle lady with kindness radiating from her soft gray eyes; Miss Hattie Platter, Miss Baur's executive secretary; Miss Mildred Benham, secretary to the general manager, and Miss Mabel Hall, whose special province was the transcript and records department. It was my good fortune to occupy a desk next to hers. She was always pleasant, kind, and courteous, never too busy to be helpful.

During the first week in the office, I seldom saw Miss Baur except when she passed my desk on her way out. Thus far, I had worked under Mrs. Benton's supervision while she was teaching me the office routine. Monday morning of the second week, however, Mrs. Benton called me to her desk and explained that from now on I would be taking dictation from Miss Baur. I was immediately thrown into a panic. My co-workers had warned me that Miss Baur "dictated like a house afire," permitted no interruptions and, what was worse, used words "you can't even find in the dictionary." I protested to Mrs. Benton that I was not yet ready for the responsibility of Miss Baur's correspondence, but she was adamant. By the time the buzzer on my desk sounded an impatient *rat-a-tat-tat*, I was virtually in a state of shock. My knees were as weak as my will, but I picked up my shorthand notebook with a show of confidence I was far from feeling and hurried into Miss Baur's private office. There had been nothing to fear. She immediately put me at ease and before I knew what was happening I was taking dictation "like a house afire." Fortunately, she didn't use any words not available in the dictionary.

Before this first summer at the Conservatory had come to an end, we were saddened by the death of our beloved Mrs. Benton. Miss Annie Howard, who was at that time dean of women, was appointed to succeed her in the position of registrar. Mrs. Inez Perrin Day was then named by Miss Baur as the new dean of women.

Dr. John Hoffmann described Miss Howard as "interesting and amazing," and not without reason. She was a versatile woman, gifted with unusual intelligence and a keen wit. Frank, outspoken, sometimes caustic, she was invariably fair and impartial. Her tartness of tongue was one of her most endearing qualities, masking a warmhearted, sympathetic nature, which she went to great lengths to conceal. Candid and direct in all her dealings, she left no doubt as to her position on any issue. "She spoke the truth or nothing at all," said Miss Marionbelle Blocksom, assistant dean of women. Miss Howard had served the Conservatory in a number of capacities, first as Miss Clara Baur's personal secretary, and later as dean of women. Miss Howard retired in June, 1930, and returned to her home in Henderson, Kentucky.

The Conservatory business office was in the charge of Miss Baur's cousin, George A. Baur, a sprightly little man with a ruddy complexion and the distinctive blue eyes of the Baurs. He discharged the duties of his office with neatness and efficiency, assisted by Miss Flay Butler and Miss Alice Leeds. Miss Butler spoke of him recently. "He was the most considerate person in the world to work for," she said, "and probably had the most thankless job in the entire school." Miss Blocksom recalls that "Mr. George" had a whimsical sense of humor and was "fond of playing practical jokes." Like most of his family, George Baur was talented musically. He was an accomplished cellist and played with the leading ensemble groups in the Queen City. He also served for many years as the choir director of the Third German Methodist Church, located at McMicken Avenue and Walnut Street in Cincinnati. Like his cousin, Bertha, he had a quick temper, and when he was angry it was time to look for the nearest exit.

In the autumn of 1924, Miss Grace Underhill, an attractive, career-minded young Cincinnatian, joined the Conservatory office staff as secretary to the general manager. As the school expanded and the enrollment increased, additional office personnel were needed. Misses Christine Benjamin, Bertha Stahl, and Ruth Hall, Mabel's "little" sister, were added to the staff.

We (the secretaries) had an almost infallible way of recognizing Miss Baur's footfall as she came down the corridor on her way to her private office. For some reason, she had her shoe heels reinforced with metal lifts rather than rubber, and the clickety-clack of the metal against the marble floor gave ample warning of her approach. As soon as we heard her footsteps beating out a firm tattoo, all small talk abruptly ceased and there was a great flurry of activity. Typewriters clattered at a furious pace and heads bent studiously over paperwork in unaccustomed devotion. It was not that we were afraid of Miss Baur, or that we stood in awe of her, even though, on occasion, she could be a formidable person; the fact is that we held her in high esteem and were reluctant to have her find us neglecting our work.

During these busy, productive years, Miss Baur's mail was so heavy it was impossible for her to read every letter. Many former students, wishing to keep her informed of their musical careers, would write at length of their experiences. One of my duties was to read these long and often interesting letters, sort out the pertinent facts and give her a typed condensation. A now-famous opera singer, a Conservatory graduate, would be surprised and perhaps disappointed to learn that one of her eight-page letters was reduced to three short paragraphs before it reached Miss Baur's desk. She was genuinely interested in these young artists struggling for recognition in the music world, and no letter went unanswered.

7

Since there was no outside door to Miss Baur's private office, she was obliged to come through the front office past the secretaries' desks to reach her own. A constant stream of celebrities from all walks of life and of many nationalities came to call on her and to look over the Conservatory. This made the front office a very fascinating place to be and, because Miss Baur was a gracious, understanding person, she usually paused briefly to introduce the office personnel to the visitor, giving us the rare privilege of meeting the musical elite of our time.

One occasion was especially memorable. During one of Paderewski's concert appearances in Cincinnati, we learned that he was to have lunch that day with Miss Baur. For once, not one member of the office force found it necessary to be absent from her desk. No one wanted to miss the opportunity of meeting the world's most famous pianist. The morning dragged on, but he did not appear. Finally, noon came, the lunch bell rang, and still he had not arrived. We were barely seated in the dining hall when Miss Baur appeared in the doorway with the one, the only, Paderewski. As if on cue, the entire student body arose as one man to welcome the great Polish master. Miss Baur made a short, informal introduction, Paderewski smiled, bowed in the courtly continental manner and, without a word, followed Miss Baur into her private dining room. The great moment had come and gone.

Meeting and entertaining celebrities was, for Miss Baur, all in a day's work, but because of her understanding of young people, she realized that for the student it was a new and exciting experience. "Young people are basically the same in every generation," she once said. "They differ only in outward appearance." To prove her point, she related an incident that occurred when young Artur Rubenstein came to call on Miss Clara. He was only eighteen years of age, but was already making a name as a brilliant young artist. He was in the Queen City for a few days prior to his appearance at the Grand Opera House. When the rumor spread through the school that the young pianist was at that very moment in the drawing room, ceremony was tossed to the winds, and several hundred girls noisily assembled in front of the door, much to Miss Clara's embarrassment. With vigorous hand-clapping they demanded that he come forth and play for them. At first he graciously declined, saying that he had a sore thumb. In vain did Miss Clara explain that Mr. Rubenstein played only in regularly scheduled concerts. The clamor only increased, and the applause grew so tumultuous that he was obliged, finally, to go into the concert hall where he gave a magnificent, if unscheduled, recital. After he had played several selections, young Rubenstein fled, with thunderous applause ringing in his ears.

In those strict, conventional times it would have been unthinkable for a young lady to scream, faint, or resort to tears in such a situation, but even in 1906, girls had their own way of "sending the message."

What impressed me most during those first weeks in the Conservatory office was the fact that Miss Baur seemed to know, without being told, everything that was happening. She had her finger on the pulse of every department, from the kitchen to the concert hall. Literally no decision could be made without her approval. There was one exception. George Baur made his own decisions. The bursar's neat, orderly office was his private bailiwick in which one interfered at his own peril.

Chapter II

THE TORCH IS PASSED

Those having torches will pass them on to others.

Plato

On a cold, bleak day in January of 1913, in the spacious, book-lined office of Alfred K. Nippert, prominent Cincinnati attorney, Bertha Baur waited to hear the reading of her aunt's will. Outside, large feathery snowflakes drifted lazily from a leaden sky, brushing lightly against windowpanes and muffling the sounds in the street. On the desk in front of Mr. Nippert was a legal document, neatly bound in a blue cover.

"This is the Last Will and Testament of Miss Clara Baur, of Cincinnati, Hamilton County, Ohio," he said, and began to read.

> I give, devise and bequeath to my beloved niece, Bertha Baur, who for many years has been my faithful co-worker in the management and development of the Cincinnati Conservatory of Music, founded by me in the City of Cincinnati in the year A.D. 1867, all of my property, real, personal and mixed. . . .[1]

As she listened, Bertha Baur was carried back across the years to a warm, sunny day in June, 1876, when she had arrived in Cincinnati to spend the summer with Aunt Clara. She was only seventeen, and the visit had been a gift from her parents to mark her recent graduation from the Ann Arbor (Michigan) High School. She had ambitious plans for entering the University of Michigan to prepare for a career in medicine, but her aunt had needed someone to assist her in the management of her rapidly-growing music school and the position had been urged upon Bertha. Where had the years gone? It seemed only yesterday. "Time has rushed by like a millrace," she mused, "and youthful dreams have given place to stern reality."

She was lost now in contemplation, and scenes from those

10

early years crowded in upon her mind, blotting out the present. The voice of her attorney receded into an indistinct murmur. She was remembering the little studio on West Seventh Street where the Conservatory had its modest beginning; the incomparable Schumann-Heink singing in the May Festival; the young pianist, Artur Rubenstein, playing an impromptu concert in the Conservatory recital hall. One scene, more vivid than all the others, re-appeared with distressing clarity: Aunt Clara, sitting at her rosewood desk, her blue eyes grave and serious, speaking earnestly of sacrifice, loyalty, and duty to one's family, while she, Bertha, remained silent, her fingers tightly gripped together, the knuckles white with strain. The meaning of Aunt Clara's words was clear. Marriage, for her, would not be possible so long as she was needed in the school.

As if returning from a long journey, she became aware that the reading was finished and Mr. Nippert was offering his congratulations upon her new position as director. With an effort she brought the room back into focus. When all legal matters had been concluded, she hurried back to her desk where important matters awaited her attention. She would have little time for the luxury of looking back.

Bertha Baur had known for many years that she would succeed her aunt as director of the Cincinnati Conservatory of Music. Since her eighteenth year she had been administrative assistant to "Miss Clara" (as she was affectionately known in Cincinnati), and they had worked together in perfect accord. Now, without warning, she was to assume the full responsibility. Was it only a short month ago that she had received the fatal message that her aunt was dead? Every detail of that tragic morning was indelibly stamped upon the pages of her memory. . . .

It was December 18, 1912. She was in the harbor of New York City en route to Europe to engage a voice teacher for the artist faculty. The day was clear and cold, the wind brisk and bracing. The big, glittering liner was under full steam and the tugs were ready to convoy her out to sea. The time of departure was imminent and the decks resounded with the crescendo of increased activity. The pier was crowded and the passengers were in a holiday mood. Christmas was only one week away.

In her cabin Bertha Baur was chatting with friends who had come to wish her bon voyage. There was a knock at the door, and a messenger handed her a telegram. She was to return at once to Cincinnati. Miss Clara Baur had died that morning following a heart attack. Hastily she retrieved her baggage and made her way down the gangplank minutes before the "all ashore."

The train bringing her back to Cincinnati hurled itself across mountains, through cities and hamlets, and past abandoned coal mines, their elevator shafts starkly outlined against the fading sky. The long night lay ahead. It would be morning before they reached the rich meadows and broad, fertile farmlands of Ohio.

She stared pensively out of the train window as the sun declined and purple shadows deepened into twilight. She recalled with nostalgia and not a little pain the years she and Miss Clara had worked together to give security and prestige to the school: their mutual hardships, their shared dreams, disappointments, joys and sorrows, and the unexpected "windfalls" that had made it possible to keep the Conservatory in operation. She remembered with gratitude those loyal co-workers and faithful friends who had helped them guide the school through its darkest days: William S. Rowe, president of the First National Bank; David Gamble, of the Procter & Gamble Company; Dr. Frank H. Nelson, rector of Christ Church; Frederic Shailer Evans, head of the piano department; and many other business and professional men and patrons of the arts. She smiled when she thought of Miss Annie Howard, Miss Clara's personal secretary, whose wry sense of humor and sharp, pithy remarks had often put her problems in proper perspective.

"Even with steadfast friends and loyal colleagues to help me," she mused, "the full responsibility will now be mine." Unconsciously, she straightened her slender shoulders, mentally strapping on the heavy load.

Thus did memory shuttle back and forth like the threads in a weaver's loom, revealing the fabric of her life: bright days, gray days, sunshine, and shadow. Following swiftly in succession, they had formed the pattern of her more than thirty-five years of devoted service to the Cincinnati Conservatory of Music.

Bertha Baur was the first child of the Reverend Emil Gottlieb Ludwig Baur and Johanna Christina Bertha (Herzer) Baur. She was born on July 17, 1858, in Cleveland, Ohio, where her father was serving an interim pastorate in the German Methodist Church of that city.[2]

It was apparent from the very first that this new member of the Baur family was no ordinary child. Active, precocious and willful, she quickly showed signs of unusual intelligence and was a source of great pride to her scholarly father, who boasted of her achievements to anyone who would listen. This inordinate pride caused him to spoil her outrageously. She soon learned that her father was putty in her tiny hands, a discovery she was not reluctant to use in gaining her own ends. With her perky red-gold curls, clear blue eyes, and dimpled smile, she captivated everyone who came within her orbit.

Bertha Baur came into the world during one of the most interesting and exciting periods in Cleveland's history. With its natural harbors and shipping facilities, it had become a busy transportation center, and was just beginning to realize its potential in manufacturing, commerce, and industry. The "Soo" (Sault Sainte Marie) Canal had been completed in 1855 and, a year or two before, residents of Cleveland had watched as the first train puffed into their city. The War Between the States was imminent. Preparations for the conflict that was sure to come had created a thriving market for the matériel of war. As the population increased, the town spread out in all directions. Cleveland's underground was helping hundreds of fugitive slaves to escape to the North. Emil Baur was thought to have been active in this movement, but members of the Baur family discount this as legend.

Bertha Baur's father, Emil Gottlieb Ludwig Baur, was born on February 2, 1831, in Haiterbach, near Stuttgart, in the Königreich of Württemberg, Germany. He was the second son of George William Ludwig Baur, a Lutheran clergyman, and Maria Fredericka (Finke) Baur.[3] With his older brother, Theodor, Emil emigrated to the United States early in the year 1848. At that time, Germany was in a turmoil of internal strife, dissension, and political upheavel, threatening momentarily to explode into revolution. In such an event, the Baur brothers would not have been able to escape conscription into the army because of Germany's compulsory draft laws. Abhorring the thought of war and bloodshed, Emil and Theodor left their native country rather than be forced into a conflict which they could not in conscience support. They believed that the United States, with its rapidly growing population, its vast, undeveloped regions, and its abundant resources, afforded the best opportunities and offered the greatest challenge. Their father seems not to have discouraged his sons in this venture, but rather to have given them his blessing.

Strangely, upon reaching the United States, the Baur brothers each went his separate way. Theodor, an enterprising young man with a talent for business, chose Cincinnati, at that time the undisputed center of commerce and industry in the Midwest. As early as 1850, his name is prominently mentioned by Cincinnati historians in connection with the financial institutions of the city. Early in his residence in Cincinnati he became affiliated with Espy, Heidelbach and Company (later, a branch was established in the name of Heidelbach, Baur and Company.), a well-known banking firm. Through a series of mergers and consolidations, this company eventually became The First National Bank of Cincinnati. Theodor Baur was appointed manager of the foreign exchange department and, upon his death, his son Theodor, Jr., succeeded him in this position. In this capacity, he was in charge of all the Cincinnati business of the large steamship companies for which The First National Bank had the agencies.

Emulating his father's example, Emil entered the ministry, dedicating his time and efforts to alleviating the evils of social injustice and to the mitigation of poverty and suffering among the poor and underprivileged. He dreamed of a social and economic order in which every man would be granted an equal opportunity to make the most of whatever talent he possessed. Emil Baur's one burning desire was to be instrumental in making this dream a reality.

After a short stay in Cincinnati, he settled in Pittsburgh, Pennsylvania, serving as a missionary in the slum district of that city. Seeing firsthand the shocking privations, the destitution, and the terrible distress of these unfortunate people, he undertook to serve not only as their spiritual adviser, but to minister to their physical and material needs as well.

In the meantime, the young clergyman had married Johanna Christina Bertha Herzer, from Detroit, Michigan, who, like her husband, was deeply involved in missionary work among the needy and the disadvantaged. Shortly after their marriage, he was asked to accept a temporary assignment as pastor of the German Methodist Church in Cleveland. It was there, in the little parsonage at 90 Prospect Street, that their first child, Bertha, was born.

Chapter III

AN ILLUSTRIOUS LINEAGE

It is indeed desirable to be
well descended, but the glory belongs
to our ancestors.

Plutarch

The Baur Family, one of the oldest and most respected families in Germany, traces its lineage back to the fifteenth century. The first written document concerns one Barttolomaüs Baur, a minister of the Gospel, who was born in the town of Reütlingen in 1518.

According to the Chronicles of Reütlingen, the Reverend Baur was a "devout, Godly and courageous man who left his native town rather than commit the sin of apostasy" and preach what he considered "the Pope's false doctrine." At some time during his ministry he had rejected the teachings of the Church of Rome to become a disciple of Martin Luther. Such an action required a special kind of courage when, in those troublesome times, to defy the authority of the Catholic Church was to risk torture on the rack or death at the stake.

This was the time of the Reformation. Germany had become the theatre of a religious conflict that threatened intermittently to flare into open rebellion. There was internal strife, dissension, and persecution. The country was divided into more than three hundred splinter states, and fragmentation increased as Luthernism spread. Feelings of unrest and resentment grew and tempers smoldered. After a long period of procrastination, Karl V offered a compromise which he hoped would be acceptable to the followers of Martin Luther and to the Church of Rome. Known as "The Interim," it was satisfactory to neither side, and only served to widen the breach.

"Bartle" Baur, as he was known to his friends, refused to accept the hated Interim, continuing openly to teach the tenets

16

of Luthernism and, by his defiance, placed his life in jeopardy. As the conflict raged, his position grew more and more precarious. He dared not remain in Reütlingen, preferring to live in exile rather than to forsake his convictions. The Baur genealogy says that "spontaneous he left the town. . . . He set out to find a safe place and went to Leezenhofen." The Duke of Württemberg, who by this time had joined the Protestant movement, allowed him "to stay there until he died, having acquired already a place in Heaven."

For the next hundred years or more, according to family records, the descendants of Barttolomaüs Baur seem to have abandoned the Church as a profession. They went into business and prospered as merchants, guildmasters, and tradesmen in and near the cities of Reütlingen and Stuttgart. Not until the late seventeenth century was this pattern broken. Andrew Baur, the son of John Christopher Baur, became an attorney and counselor at law and distinguished himself in politics. In 1675 he married Regina Laütenberger, the daughter of the *bürger-meister* (or mayor) or Reütlingen. Andrew's only son, Christian, did not follow his father's profession. He entered the world of business as a textile manufacturer and, a few years later, married the daughter of the village baker.

In succeeding years, the clerical tradition seems to have reasserted itself, the Baur sons devoting themselves either to the ministry or to the teaching profession. Perhaps the most illustrious educator of the Baur family in Germany was the theologian Ferdinand Christian Baur. He was born in June 21, 1793, in the neighborhood of Cannstadt, where his father was pastor of a Lutheran church. After completing the prescribed course of study at the well-known Blaubeuran Seminary, he entered the University of Tübingen, from which he graduated in 1809. For two years he taught at the Blaubeuran Seminary, then returned to Tübingen, occupying the first chair of theology until his death thirty-four years later. He is the author of an impressive number of treatises on the origin of religion, many of them in use today in seminaries and schools of religion. The name of Ferdinand Christian Baur is cherished as that of one of the greatest theologians of all time.

In the year 1796, another member of the Baur family entered

the field of education. George Ludwig, son of John George and Marie Elizabeth (Hess) Baur, and the grandson of Christian Baur, assumed the position of rector of the high school at Pfüllingen. He was married to Henricka Saloma Kurtz, the daughter of Johannes Kurtz, a senator at Zinkgeiser. To this union were born four boys and two girls. The second son, George William Ludwig Baur, entered the ministry, preaching first at Haiterbach, then at Reütlingen, and finally at Stuttgart. This Baur ancestor became Bertha Baur's grandfather. He was thrice married. To his first wife, Maria Fredericka (Finke) Baur, were born four children: Theodor (1828), Emil Gottlieb (1831), Augusta (1833), and Clara (1835). Maria Fredericka died when Clara was born.

To the Reverend Baur's second marriage three children were born: Louis, Louise, and Julia; the last-named child died at the age of fifteen. Not much is known of the second wife except that her surname was Kammerer. The third marriage was to Fredericka Hoerner, the daughter of a parson at Brenz. Only one child was born of this union, a son, Herman, who came to the United States in 1870 and settled in St. Louis, Missouri, where he was married to Maria Hezel, the daughter of a physician.[1]

In more recent years, other Baur sons have distingished themselves as educators. Dr. Paul Victor Christopher Baur (1872-1951), an eminent archaeologist, was associate professor of archaeology at Yale University from 1902 until 1940, when he became professor emeritus.

Dr. Baur was born in Cincinnati, the son of Theodor Baur, Sr. After graduating from the University of Cincinnati in 1894, he went to Heidelberg University for further study where, in 1900, he received his Ph.D. He will be remembered for his fine work, *Centaurs in Ancient Art: the Archaic Period* (Berlin, 1912), and for his catalog of the Rebecca Darlington Stoddard Collection of Greek and Italian vases at Yale University (New Haven, 1922). With Rostovtzeff, Dr. Baur edited the first and second reports of the excavations of Dura-Europos, and with Rostovtzeff and Bellinger, the third and fourth. Upon his death on June 5, 1951, the *American Journal of Archaeology* stated: "He [Dr. Baur] was one of the last of the older group of teachers and scholars to whose efforts and encouragement is due the large growth in interest and study witnessed in the profession of archaeology."[2]

A notable exception to this long line of clergymen and educators was Count General Henri Gratien Bertrand, one of Napoleon's most trusted officers. Count General Bertrand is the "mystery man" of the Baur family. His name does not appear in the genealogy; however, Mrs. Robert Morse (Wanda Constance Baur, daughter of Bertrand Baur),[3] states that "this is not just a family legend. I have heard my father say many times that he was named in honor of our kinsman, Count Henri Bertrand." Whether this kinship came through the maternal or the paternal line is not known.

Count General Henri Gratien Bertrand was born in Chateauroux, France, on March 28, 1773, and died on January 31, 1884, in the city of his birth. Upon Napoleon's banishment to the Isle of St. Helena, Count General Bertrand, who had been master of the palace, was one of the four officers chosen to accompany him into exile. Years later, Napoleon's body was disinterred from its burial place in St. Helena and brought back to Paris for entombment under the dome of the Invalides. At the last rites, Count Bertrand was selected for the honor of placing Napoleon's sword upon the casket. Count Bertrand is also entombed in the Invalides near the last resting place of his beloved emperor.

On the maternal side, Bertha Baur's ancestors hailed from Saxony, the German state that gave to the world such masters of music as Handel and Schumann.

The Herzers were descended from a long line of ancient Teutonic peoples who were farmers, foresters, and pomologists. They owned and cultivated their own land as far back as Frederick the Wise, when serfdom had been abolished.

In 1849 Christoph F. Herzer, with his wife, Wilhelmina, and their six children, Fred, Herman, Gustav, Richard, Bertha, and Wilhelmine, left his ancestral acres and emigrated to the United States.[4] Miriam (Otto) Kockritz, a direct descendant of this family, discussed the reason for such a drastic step.

"It is entirely possible," Mrs. Kockritz said, "that the Herzers, who were peaceful farmer folk, abandoned their home

19

and country rather than be conscripted into the army."[5]

Internal strife had been prevalent in Saxony for some time. The country was ripe for rebellion. The people were dissatisfied with certain mandates imposed upon them by Frederick Augustus II, and public demonstrations had taken place in Dresden in May, 1849. The people had seized the town and barricaded the streets. After two days of fierce fighting, the uprising was quelled, but only after the arrival of Prussian troops. The presence of Prussian soldiers boded no good for the Saxons, especially the farmers, who feared that their sons would be conscripted into the army and their crops confiscated to feed the invaders. Persecution was becoming acute and many Saxons, like Christoph Herzer, watched the Prussian oppressors with growing anxiety and, feeling the situation intolerable, left their homes and fled to other countries rather than submit to confiscation and compulsory military service.

It is interesting historically to note that Richard Wagner, who gave to the world such sublime music, was in Dresden during this uprising, not composing music, but writing inflammatory articles against the Prussian regime. When the revolution broke out, a warrant was issued for his arrest, but he escaped to Weimar where, with the help of his friend, Franz Liszt, he was spirited across the border to safety.

Shortly after his arrival in the United States, Christoph Herzer settled his family on a farm near Francisco, Michigan. Eight years later, his daughter Bertha met and married a young missionary clergyman, the Reverend Emil Gottlieb Baur.

Herman, the second son of Christoph and Wilhelmina Herzer, gifted with unusual intelligence, was destined to become nationally known in America as a geologist and paleontologist. He was born in Neustadt, Saxony, and was eleven years old when he was brought to the United States. He died on May 20, 1912. As a young man, Herman Herzer worked in New York City for a few years, then returned to Michigan and married Miss Pauline Seiberlich, also a native of Germany. He preached in several cities in the East before being appointed superintendent of the Berea (Ohio) Orphanage. He also served as a district superintendent of the German Methodist Church Conference of Ohio.

"Geology was his hobby," said his son, August Scheffel

("Scheff") Herzer, of Zanesville, Ohio. He also stated that some of his father's specimens are on display in the National Museum in Washington, D.C.[6]

Mrs. Kockritz, whose mother, Cornelia (Herzer) Otto, was Dr. Herzer's youngest daughter, recently reminisced about her distinguished grandfather. "It is not generally known," she said, "that my grandfather was also a very fine taxidermist. He lived with us during the last years of his life, and brought with him a fascinating collection of mounted birds." Mrs. Kockritz remembers vividly a beautiful peacock which her grandfather preserved and mounted. "Peacocks are supposed to be bad luck," she mused, "but the Herzer family was not superstitious." She also recalls that her family had a collection of Dr. Herzer's choice rock specimens in which, as a child, she had a great interest.

Dr. Herzer was among the first to recognize the historical and scientific significance of fossils and rock formations. He devoted many years of patient and painstaking research to this field. He was a familiar and beloved figure, with his pick and shovel, digging for fossils in the Berea Grit and the limestone formations. One of his discoveries, an important fossil, was named in his honor: *Dinichthsys Hertzeri* (Hertzer's Terrible Fish).[7]

From 1872 until 1882 Dr. Herzer served German Wallace College as lecturer in natural science. His rock collection was housed on the campus of Baldwin-Wallace College in a museum which bore his name and of which he was curator.

In 1966 Herman Herzer's great-great-grandson, Robert Fawcett, Jr., was present at the ground-breaking ceremony for a new life and earth science building for Baldwin-Wallace College. He watched as Dr. Herzer's famous pick and several of his choice specimens were sealed into the cornerstone of this important new building. When it was completed and dedicated on Founder's Day, October 19, 1967, Robert Fawcett, Jr., together with his grandmother, Mrs. Herman A. Herzer, unveiled the plaque honoring this great pioneer in the study of the earth sciences. It bears the legend: Dr. Herman Herzer, Lecturer in Natural Science, 1872-1882. Lecturer and Curator of the Geological Museum 1886-1908. This remarkable scholar, whose geological collections won national renown, pioneered in the study of the earth sciences of the college and helped build an early tradition for great teaching.[8]

Mrs. Dorothy M. McKelvy, as historian at Baldwin-Wallace College, has referred to Dr. Herzer as "that inspired soul who collected many valuable fossils." She also stated that he was a member of the Ohio Academy of Science and was employed in the service of the Geological Survey of Ohio and Kentucky.

The Herzer genealogy reveals that this famous scientist was a brother of Johanna Christina Bertha (Herzer) Baur and the uncle of Bertha Baur.

Chapter IV

ORA ET LABORA—THE IMPOSSIBLE DREAM

He whom a dream hath possessed
knoweth no more of doubting. . . .
Shaemas O'Sheel, *He Whom a Dream hath Possessed*

When Bertha was almost two years of age, Emil Baur, with his wife and small daughter, returned to Pittsburgh to resume his missionary ministry in the tenement district. A few months afterward, their second child, a son, was born. He was named Bertrand.

While serving the Cleveland pastorate, Emil Baur had been unable to forget the plight of the slum dwellers. He was haunted by the gaunt faces of hunger, the uncomprehending gaze of starving children, and the bewildered looks of their parents. The community was made up of the poor and unemployed, mostly immigrants of German origin, who had come to the United States to escape the hardships and privations of war in their own country. Many of them had fled with very little more than the clothes they were wearing, leaving all their worldly possessions behind. The young clergyman felt that here was a real challenge and an opportunity for service. Searching for a way to improve the lot of these unfortunate people, he conceived the idea of establishing a religious communal society where opportunity would be equal for all. Assets would be consolidated, labor and earnings shared equally, and all property jointly held.

"My grandfather believed that a Christian cooperative society, such as he had in mind, would provide a wholesome and satisfying life for the impoverished of the city's slums," said Mrs. Morse. "He worked all of his life to accomplish this. How these people repaid him is one of the saddest chapters in his life."

After months of careful searching, planning, and negotiating, a large tract of land was found along the shore of Lake Huron in Michigan's "thumb" area: an untamed, virgin wilderness where no white man had lived before. Cultivated land was scarce as well as expensive and this was the best obtainable with the funds they had been able to procure. In fact, it was necessary to borrow a large sum of money with which to finance the purchase of the land. Here they would establish their colony: the first cooperative society in the state of Michigan.

Emil Baur's inspiration for this undertaking was the success of the *Harmonists*, a communal colony near Economy (now Ambridge), Pennsylvania. Organized in 1804, this pioneer colony had been able to accumulate considerable holdings, mainly in farmlands and livestock. He was also influenced by another communal group known as *Brook Farm*, located at Roxbury, Massachusetts, in which his friend Nathaniel Hawthorne was a leading spirit. The money with which to buy the land in Michigan was borrowed from the *Harmonists*, Emil Baur making himself largely responsible for the repayment of the loan. Years later, Mrs. Morse was to say: "My grandfather spent his entire life working to repay this debt." The corporate name of the colony was to be *The Christian German Agricultural and Benevolent Society of Ora et Labora*—"pray and work." It was usually referred to, however, simply as *Ora Labora*.[1]

It was while Emil Baur was in Detroit working out the plans for the founding of the colony that he met his future bride, a spirited young lady from Francisco, Michigan, and a recent graduate of the Young Ladies' Academy. He lost no time in persuading her to become his wife. The year was 1857. The Herzer genealogy gives her age as seventeen.

During this time, plans were being perfected for the transfer of the colonists from Pittsburgh to their new home on the shore of Lake Huron. Letters in the possession of Mrs. Morse indicate that Reverend Baur made many trips to Ann Arbor, Saginaw, and Detroit before the final details of the purchase were completed. In his brief history of the colony, Emil Baur states: "Messrs. Herman and Ed Goeschel and Reverend Mr. Maenz, of East Saginaw, selected the location on Wild Fowl Bay. The rest of the members . . . had perfect confidence in the judgment of these candid men."[2]

At length, all was in readiness. The time had come to take

possession of the land. The date was December 2, 1862.[3] The colonists sailed from Port Huron on a schooner and were caught in a sudden storm that threatened to engulf them. Sheets of gust-driven rain and sleet slashed at the small craft, and for a time they despaired of reaching their destination. As suddenly as it had come, however, the rain ceased, the waters grew calm, and the settlers were able to put in to shore. More than fifty families had embarked on this journey into the unknown.

Legend says that the colonists had taken an oath never to leave their wilderness homes and, as a pledge of their good faith, an altar was built of stones taken from the bay. Each colonist placed a stone on the pile until the altar was complete. The basis for this legend is found in Article Fourteen of the Constitution of the colony, which provided:

> To the triune God an altar shall be built to the praise of His glorious name in remembrance of our covenant. This altar shall be built of stones which shall be taken out of the water of our Bay [Wild Fowl Bay]. Every person that is admitted into full membership of our Society shall add a stone to this altar before such person is admitted to full connection.[4]

In her manuscript, *Ora Labora*, Mrs. Lela Puffer, of Flint, Michigan, states: "The altar, if it ever existed, is lost under the shifting sands of the shore of Lake Huron."

During the first months when Emil Baur was struggling against almost overwhelming odds to establish the colony, "his wife's sympathetic parents sent hogsheads of clothes and food, which they gave freely to all . . . bravely Mrs. Baur carried on, raising her family, holding school for the children, and lending her home to be used as a church."[5]

"The village of *Ora Labora* is regularly laid out in squares with wide streets, and the colonists have adopted a good old custom of the fatherland, adorning the streets with fruit trees," wrote the editor of the *Huron News* in 1865. "We understand that each newcomer is given forty acres of land."

Although Bertha Baur was only four-and-a-half years of age when the move was made from Pittsburgh to the Michigan woods, the experience made a lasting impression upon her. From the windows of the rambling old parsonage in Pittsburgh, she could see the long, heavily laden barges inch their way into the harbor and hear the whistle of the steamboats on the river. In the remote region of Michigan's lower peninsula, it is doubtful if any craft put in to shore. Only the distant echo of a woodman's axe, deep in the dense forest, or the call of the curlew and the honking of wild geese broke the silence as the birds fed in the shallow waters along the bay.

In spite of the solitude and the austerity of her surroundings, Bertha Baur's childhood was happy and rewarding. In the springtime, rare and beautiful wild flowers grew in profusion, thrushes sang in the nearby thickets, and the air was pungent with the scent of pine trees. In the autumn, she thrilled to the grace and symmetry of the flocks of migratory birds flying majestically over the bay on their way to wintering grounds in the South. But most of all, she loved the still, mysterious forest, blanketed with giant trees as far as the eye could see. It was here in this woodland setting that the perceptive little girl learned to love and respect nature in all of its varied moods.

In the first few months, the pioneer colonists endured untold hardships, dangers, and privations. Swamp fever and pneumonia took a heavy toll. It was necessary for the children, as well as the livestock, to be constantly protected from predatory animals: wolves, bears, and panthers that roamed the nearby woods. At night all windows and doors had to be locked and barred against the furtive attacks of these nocturnal prowlers. Necessities of life were scarce. Food had to be grown and harvested in their fields; clothing and household furnishings were fashioned by their own hands. The nearest town was Bay City and could be reached only by walking or on horseback.

In the beginning, when only a few of the buildings had been erected, the Baur home was the social and educational center of the settlement. The children attended school, church services were conducted, and baptismal and wedding ceremonies were performed in the Baurs' living room.

After many months of hard work, most of the communal buildings had been completed: a church, a post office, a community meetinghouse, and the village store. A monetary system had been established and trade was conducted at the general store through the medium of "greenbacks" that were made of pasteboard.

Yet in spite of the improved conditions, the colonists were not satisfied. There was suspicion, unrest, and discontent. They grumbled against Emil Baur, accusing him of "stealing everything" and "wasting the money." On one occasion they even tried to fell a tree on him, but he was warned in time by his secretary, Louis Foul.[6]

In 1868 the brave little colony of *Ora Labora* had to be disbanded. The War Between the States had depleted the ranks of its young, able-bodied men, leaving only the very old and the very young. In 1863, when the government began conscription, the fate of *Ora Labora* was sealed. Unable to pay for substitutes (which was allowed by law), the colony became so decimated that it was impossible to carry on the work of the community. To Emil Baur, the failure of his cherished dream was a shattering experience. Today, only a few scarred and broken bricks and the tangled roots of fruit trees mark the site of the heroic struggle for which Emil Baur gave the better part of his life. Even in the face of crushing disappointment, his faith did not waver, nor did his courage fail. To the end of his life Emil Baur worked unceasingly to give assistance to those who had shared with him in this noble experiment.

Although his dream of justice and equality for all men was incapable of fulfillment in the circumstances of time and place, such an outpouring of love and compassion cannot be said to have failed. Mrs. Morse put it aptly when she said, "Even though the experiment was outwardly a failure, my grandfather's life has been an influence for good in the subsequent history of that part of Michigan."

Henry David Thoreau has written of the exceptional man who "steps out confidently in the direction of his dream."[7] Such a man was Emil Baur.

Chapter V

GROWING UP IN ANN ARBOR

Sweet childish days, that
were as long
As twenty days are now.
William Wordsworth, "To a Butterfly"

A few years before the final curtain closed on the brief but thrilling drama of *Ora Labora*, the Reverend Baur had moved his family to Ann Arbor where he maintained a permanent home, and where he later accepted a position as professor of Germanic languages in the high school. It is probable that this appointment was made upon the recommendation of Dr. E. O. Haven, president of the University of Michigan during this time and one of Emil Baur's closest friends.

To accommodate their growing family, the Baurs had bought a large, two-story frame house located on Dexter Road. It was set well back from the main thoroughfare, sheltered by tall cedars, oaks, and maples. With its high ceilings, wide windows, and huge fireplaces, the house was in perfect accord with its rural surroundings. Only a mile from the city limits of Ann Arbor, the tract afforded sufficient acreage for Professor Baur to pursue his favorite hobby, the growing of fruit trees, which he cultivated after school hours when his teaching duties were finished for the day. He also found time to cultivate several varities of strawberries, raspberries, and grapes. From his sweet Concord grapes he made wine which he advertised as "especially adapted for sacramental purposes and for convalescents, as fermentation was stopped early."[1] Said Mrs. Morse: "My grandfather was far ahead of his time in foreseeing that prohibition would fail." In a memorandum (now in possession of Mrs. Morse), he set down his thoughts on the subject, with Biblical references to reinforce his opinions.

The Baur's home life on Dexter Road was complicated and

busy. On the ground floor of the spacious farmhouse, the Reverend Baur had his study. The windows looked out on the west lawn and beyond to the fruit trees and grape arbors. In the evenings, Bertha and her father would read and study together. He would assist her in her school assignments and she, in turn, would listen with a critical ear to the articles he was preparing for current magazines. In addition to his classes at the high school, Professor Baur (as he was called in Ann Arbor) was a regular contributor to a number of publications in both the English and German languages. His articles in *Der Christliche Apologete*[2] were widely read and favorably received.

In the long winter evenings, when the earth lay silent and frozen under a soft white blanket of snow, reading aloud became the custom in the Baur family. Sitting at his desk in his comfortable old brown leather chair, Professor Baur would gather his children around an open fire of blazing logs and read aloud from the Bible, Shakespeare, and other classics, sometimes in English, sometimes in German. Almost as soon as she was able to talk, Bertha Baur was bilingual, an accomplishment which proved to be of inestimable value in later life. She was an omnivorous reader and, long before she had finished high school, she had read everything in her father's well-stocked library, including books on religion, history, and philosophy. Thanks to their parents, who had themselves enjoyed unusual educational opportunities, the Baur children were surrounded by an intellectual and cultural atmosphere that was rare in the 1800s.

As the Baur children grew up, other happy memories were stored in their hearts: picnics in summer, nutting parties in the autumn, and hayrides under a harvest moon. In winter they coasted down snow-covered slopes, coming in from the cold to feast on mugs of hot chocolate and to pop corn and roast chestnuts before the large stone fireplace in Professor Baur's study.[3] Miss Baur often spoke with nostalgia of those carefree days.

While in the midst of their busy and happy life in the pleasant, gracious home on Dexter Road, the dark shadow of death fell across the threshold, bringing to this large, devoted family its first great loss. In October, 1869, when the chill autumn rains began to fall and the harsh winds from the north lashed the leaves from the trees, little Augusta, not quite three years of age, died after a brief illness. Then, almost a year later, small Clara followed her sister in death. When Bertrand Baur was quite an old man, his daughter, Wanda Baur Morse, accompanied him on a "sentimental journey" to the old home where he had spent so many happy days. Of this visit, Mrs. Morse said: "My father spoke sadly of 'little Clara' [as she was called], pointing out the room where she had died in his arms." Besides Bertha, six other children grew up in the big white house on Dexter Road: Bertrand, Herman, Emil, William, Adelbert, and Wanda Constance. Henry, the youngest of the Baur sons, lived only a few short months.

A bond of deep affection existed between Bertha and her brother William (Billy to his family and friends). Although he was not the nearest to her in chronological age, he was, nevertheless, closest to her in spirit, understanding, and interests. Of all her brothers he was her favorite. Through the years, they kept up a lively correspondence charged with youthful reminiscences as well as discussions of current events and problems of education. In 1937, Billy made the long journey from Boulder, Colorado, where he was head of the Romance languages department at the university, to spend the month of August in Cincinnati with his sister. Dr. William Baur died in 1938.

Bertha Baur graduated from Ann Arbor High School in the class of 1876. Since the office files were destroyed in a fire that swept through the school in 1904, no record of her scholarship remains. She often spoke of her school days in Ann Arbor as the happiest days of her life. It is fortunate that this was so, because she was called upon, too early in life, to take responsibilities and share burdens too heavy for young shoulders to bear. She was a young woman of rare intellectual gifts and pronounced talents, which she should have been allowed to pursue in her own way.

Upon graduating from high school, Bertha informed her startled parents that she would like to make the practice of medicine her life's work, a daring notion in the year 1876. They tried to dissuade her, but she was adamant. Her father, who could deny her nothing, finally promised that she would be permitted to enter the medical college of the University of Michigan at the beginning of the fall semester.

In the 1800s few women had the courage, even if they had the inclination, to embark upon such a career. The medical field was strictly a man's world, and brave indeed was the woman who dared breach the walls of this masculine stronghold. Gently reared young ladies obliged to earn a livelihood did so as teachers, librarians, or governesses. Speaking of this girlhood ambition, Miss Baur once said: "I would never have been intimidated by mere masculine prejudice. In fact, opposition only strengthened my determination."

Before she had made application to the University School of Medicine, however, she received a letter that completely changed the direction of her life. The letter was from her aunt, Miss Clara Baur, director of the Cincinnati Conservatory of Music, inviting her to spend the summer in the Queen City. This casual letter of invitation altered the course of Bertha Baur's life and set her feet upon a long, hard road of sacrifice, service, and prestige, the like of which she would never have dreamed: an example of the strange and devious ways in which Fate arranges a destiny.

The Cincinnati Conservatory of Music—"Miss Baur's Conservatory," as it was familiarly called in those days—was rapidly outgrowing its small space on West Seventh Street, and Miss Clara needed someone to help her in the management of the school. She urged the position upon her niece. One cannot but wonder what means of persuasion Miss Clara employed to induce this high-spirited, strong-willed young woman to give up her plans for a career in medicine to become the business manager of a small, struggling school of music. They must have been powerful ones. Miss Annie Howard believed that Miss Clara engaged in a "bit of collusion" with her brother to divert his daughter's interest from her avowed intention to enter the medical profession. Whatever the reason, Bertha Baur remained in Cincinnati to assist her aunt in the management of what came to be, in a few short years, a conservatory of international renown.

Mrs. Alice (Baur) Hodges believes that Miss Bertha remained with her aunt from a "strong sense of family loyalty." She was

31

a "duty person," Mrs. Hodges said. "With Cousin Bertha her family always came first."[4] Years later, after Miss Clara died, Miss Bertha was asked, "Why did you give up your career in medicine to choose this one?"

"Choose!" she all but snorted, "I didn't choose. I had no choice."

Chapter VI

BERTHA BAUR TAKES COMMAND

Does the road wind uphill all
the way?
Yes, to the very end.

Christina Rosetti, "Uphill"

Although more and more of the business management of the school had, through the years, devolved upon Bertha Baur, no final decisions were made without Miss Clara's approval. Until Miss Clara's death, Miss Bertha had assumed the role of a supporting player, standing in the wings awaiting her entrance cue. Now the spotlight was upon her and she was to take the center of the stage. During the early months of her leadership, she confided to Miss Annie Howard that she "felt the weight of responsibility." Yet, with the courage and determination that characterized her throughout life, she unflinchingly accepted the role into which she had been cast: a role not of her own choosing, but one to which she eventually became reconciled and which she finally came to love.

As the new owner and director of the Conservatory, Bertha Baur was singularly fortunate to have inherited a well-established institution. A staff of capable associates and devoted friends was eager to be of assistance; the school was solvent; and a faculty of more than fifty distinguished musicians gave assurance of the continuing scholastic and artistic excellence of the curriculum. The concert hall and a new dormitory for women had been completed only the year before, and plans were in the making for still greater expansion.

The piano department had such noted artists as Theodor Bohlmann, Wilhelm Kraupner, Louis Schwebel, and Frederic Shailer Evans. The violin department was directed by the incomparable Tirindelli; Dr. Edgar Stillman-Kelley, famous composer, author and musicologist, was head of the theory and

33

composition department; voice instruction was in the hands of John A. Hoffmann, Miss Frances Moses, and Harold Beckett Gibbs. Karl Otto Staps, choirmaster and organist, had charge of the choral groups. Under the direction of Mrs. Lily Hollingshead James and Miss Helen May Curtis, the department of speech and drama (listed in the catalog as "Elocution") was one of the Conservatory's greatest assets.

Miss Clara believed that the mastery of languages was a necessary part of a student's musical training and, from the beginning, emphasis was placed upon this part of the curriculum. In addition to the regular class work, four foreign language clubs had been formed: French, German, Italian, and Spanish. A prize was offered for the best performance of an original play to be presented during the year and there was great rivalry between the groups to capture this trophy. The foreign language classes were taught by Signora Tirindelli, Italian; Madame Olga Louise Sturm, German; M. Alfred Nonnez, French; and Miss Mary Perkins, Spanish. In fact, all departments were staffed by the finest talent available. Miss Clara would not be satisfied with less.

There were strong differences between Miss Bertha and her predecessor. An editorial in *Sharps and Flats*, the campus publication, commented upon these dissimilarities: "Miss Bertha Baur possesses a totally different personality from her predecessor, but one which is equally powerful, and a masterly mind of extraordinary versatility."[1]

No one would have compared the second director to the first. In temperament, in personality, and even in dress and manner, they seemed poles apart, yet a closer look would disclose many similar traits: both were motivated by the same ideals; both were conscientious, scrupulously honest, generous to a fault, and relentless in their devotion to duty. Although each was a natural leader, each achieved her goals by entirely different methods. Miss Clara, gentle, compassionate, and deeply spiritual, directed the school with kindness, patience, and prayerful persuasion. Miss Bertha, on the other hand, "grasped the nettle" with all the assurance of her dominant nature. Not for her the quiet conciliation, the thoughtful admonition. She could, and did, shout down anyone who dared cross her. She, and she alone, was in command. In spite of these dissimilarities of personality and approach, there was a bond between these two women of indomitable spirit that had nothing to do with the ties of blood. They were friends, their harmonious relationship having its basis in mutual trust, mutual respect, and understanding. "This understanding comradeship between aunt and niece was never interrupted by a discord . . . when Clara Baur died, her work did not perish with her," stated one historian. "Where she stopped in life's row, the niece, Miss Bertha Baur, stepped in, took up the burden, and valiantly set out to finish the job. How she succeeded is one of the romances in business in Cincinnati."[2]

"Seldom have two persons striving for the same goal seemed so totally unlike as Miss Clara and Miss Bertha," Miss Helen May Curtis said, "yet they shared a rare harmony of spirit and purpose."

Dr. John A. Hoffmann, who began his studies with Miss Clara when he was only fourteen years of age, was a personal friend of the Misses Baur and had been associated with them for many years. He summed up these differences in a few concise words: "Miss Clara played *pianissimo*, Miss Bertha *fortissimo*." Then he added, with a twinkle in his usually serious, gray eyes, "It might also be said of Miss Bertha that she plays *tempo rubato.*"

Among the first acts of the new director was the modifying of the stringent dormitory rules formulated by Miss Clara. During her regime, the young men on the faculty were required to take their meals at a separate table in a corner of the dining room as far removed as possible from the young ladies. Under the new regulations, they would be permitted to sit at the table of their choice. They would also be allowed on the tennis courts for "mixed doubles," properly chaperoned, of course. This could never have happened in Miss Clara's day.

Another innovation was "late leave." This meant that young ladies attending social functions would not be required to observe the ten o'clock curfew. By making special arrangements with the dean of women, they were given permission to stay out until midnight.

One of the most explosive situations with which Miss Bertha had to contend, and one which was perhaps the supreme test of her diplomatic prowess, was the task of maintaining a harmonious atmosphere among the members of the official family—highly sensitive, volatile artists from more than a half dozen different countries—living and working together in a strongly competitive profession. But she walked this tightrope with the grace of a ballerina and the agility of a juggler. If there were tensions, clashes of temperament, or professional jealousies, they were kept well below the surface. Commenting on this situation, Dorothy Hull Beatty, well-known pianist and former student of Theodor Bohlmann, said recently: "Looking back upon it now, there seem to have been few inharmonies."

One famous feud, however, is still remembered and told with amusement by Conservatory personnel who were there at the time. Miss Minnie Tracey, American operatic soprano of wide reputation and ample proportions, constantly bickered with Dr. Fery Lulek, Austrian baritone. Miss Tracey accused him of trying to lure her best pupils away from her, and Dr. Lulek, in turn, accused her of using the same tactics on his pupils. Almost daily they threatened each other with sinister imprecations and ruinous deeds. "If I ever get my hands on him," Miss Tracey would say, "I'll throttle him." And the fiery little Austrian would retaliate with sharp words and withering looks. Mr. Ray Staater, a member of the piano faculty at the time, recently reminisced about those two famous singers. "Although they could be very convincing," he said, "everyone knew that it was all in a spirit of jest. They were really the best of friends."

There were other frustrations. From time to time, there were attractive foreign teachers on the staff: sophisticated, ingratiating men with courtly, Old World manners. Flattered by the attentions of pretty American girls, some of them were not averse to indulging in lighthearted flirtations with their pupils. Most of the girls were young and impressionable. They were fascinated by the continental bow, the extravagant compliment, the foreign accent, and the European custom of handkissing, often reading into these charming but meaningless gestures more than mere formality—a circumstance made to order for mischief and, sometimes, tragedy.

Miss Baur's constant concern was the health and well-being of the young ladies entrusted to her care in the dormitories.

Although she had competent, conscientious chaperones and housemothers in attendance, she assumed the ultimate responsibility for these young students. Many of them came from small towns and rural communities, exposed for the first time in their sheltered lives to the temptations and excitement of a large city. Add to this the liberation from parental jurisdiction and a heady situation was in the making, but Bertha Baur was wise, understanding, and watchful. She was usually successful in thwarting any plans for an unscheduled evening "on the town."

In this connection, Ray Staater tells an amusing incident, which occurred during the first months of Miss Bertha's leadership. One evening, Mr. Staater inadvertently left the door of his studio unlocked. The studio also had an outside door opening onto the back campus. The same evening, three adventurous young ladies planned to leave the dormitory after the bell for "lights out" and meet their beaus for a night of dancing. Making their cautious exit through the unlocked door of Mr. Staater's studio, the girls were greeted, not by their escorts, but by no less a person than Miss Bertha Baur. Mr. Staater laughed as he recalled that Miss Bertha had a big stick which she threatened to apply where it would do the most good if such a thing happened again.

Two events during the first year of Miss Bertha's tenure of office deserve special mention: Marcian Thalberg was added to the piano faculty and Dr. Fery Lulek was engaged as a teacher of vocal culture.

Dr. Lulek had won considerable recognition in Europe before coming to the United States. His rich, sonorous voice was greatly admired by the crowned heads of Europe, and he had given command performances in the most important music centers of the world.

It was in the summer of 1912, while Miss Baur was spending the month of August with Mrs. Mary Emery at "Mariemont," her estate in Newport, that Dr. Lulek was first brought to Miss Baur's attention. Mrs. Emery, who had heard the young Viennese singer in Europe the winter before, arranged a musicale in her home to introduce him to this fashionable summer colony. On this occasion, Dr. Lulek devoted his entire program to the songs of Schubert and Brahms. "His interpretations of the German *lieder* was truly remarkable," Miss Baur said, relating the story of their first meeting. She engaged Dr. Lulek at once as a member of the Conservatory artist faculty. He was not, however, able to assume his duties until January of the next year because of prior commitments. He gave recitals in Aeolian Hall and, together with artists from the Metropolitan Opera, assisted in the music festival that opened the great Arena in Toronto, Canada. Then followed appearances in Philadelphia, Chicago, and Buffalo, and in Cincinnati under the baton of his old friend, Dr. Ernst Kunwald.

At this time, Paris music lovers were captivated by a young Russian pianist who was giving a series of concerts to distinguished audiences of that city. The *Liberté* had called his first recital "the sensational event of the musical season." Miss Baur attended his second Paris concert and was so impressed by his magnificent performance that she determined to secure him for her faculty, if at all possible. In Bertha Baur's lexicon, however, there was no such word as "if," and before she sailed for Cincinnati she had Marcian Thalberg under contract for the school year 1913-14. It speaks volumes for her powers of persuasion that she could induce this great pianist to leave his beloved Paris where he was the idol of the music world. When Bertha Baur determined to have her own way, it was the rare person who was able to resist her magnetic personality. For his part, Mr. Thalberg said that Miss Bertha Baur was by far the most distinguished American he had seen in Paris.

Few persons were aware of the complexities Bertha Baur faced in administering a school of the size and scope of the Cincinnati Conservatory of Music. In addition to the tremendous responsibilities inherent in the management, she also had to keep abreast of the constantly changing educational trends, teaching methods, and classroom procedures, and to familiarize herself with the latest compositions, music texts, and other materials in order to keep the curriculum up to date. When she left her office at the close of the day, she always carried in her briefcase pounds of reading matter that had to be examined and analyzed at home. It was characteristic of Bertha

Baur that she neither accepted nor rejected new trends without first taking the time to study and understand them. She simply had no time to do this during office hours and, with her crowded social schedule, one wonders how she found time to do any reading at all.

Competition was also becoming a factor. Other schools of music were being established and universities were beginning to open schools of music on their campuses. The Conservatory's position was so secure, however, that these conditions at no time and in no way threatened its prestige. Its very name was magic—a sort of "open sesame" for all doors in the music world.

Chapter VII

THE NEW DIRECTOR

There's not a life, or death, or
    birth,
That has a feather's weight of
    worth
Without a woman in it.
              Kate Field, "Woman's Sphere"

Perhaps this is an appropriate place to take a closer look at the woman whose hand was now guiding the destiny of this world-renowned school of music.

Bertha Baur was in her early fifties: vigorous, forceful, and assured. Her whole appearance was one of purpose and determination—a commanding figure, accustomed to giving orders and having them obeyed. She could be utterly, devastatingly charming when it pleased her, giving the impression of quiet complacency, but one had only to oppose her to dispel this illusion, for illusion it was. Anyone having the temerity to contradict her or defy her orders soon felt the chilly atmosphere of her displeasure and often the sting of a sharp rebuke. She could be rude and caustic when she chose to be, and on occasion she so chose. Her conflicting traits, sudden changes of mood, and swift flashes of temper sometimes puzzled even her closest friends.

Bertha Baur has been called "domineering and overbearing," but more often she was spoken of as "understanding and charitable." The truth is she could be each of these. Of her generosity, however, there can be no question. Even her most outspoken critics could not deny the abundance of that quality in her personality. She gave financial assistance to literally hundreds of students who otherwise could not have secured a musical education. In fact, her whole life was dedicated to shaping the musical aspirations of young artists.

Through the years Miss Baur had a number of protégés—pupils whom she considered especially gifted. Among those whose careers she watched with great interest were Pearl Besuner, Grace Divine, Susanne Fisher, and Everett Marshall, all of whom became members of the Metropolitan Opera Company; Karl Wecker, conductor of the Grand Rapids (Michigan) Symphony Orchestra, who was later appointed managing director of the Hollywood Bowl; Jane Froman, star of radio, television, and musical theatre; A. Lehman Engel, noted composer, author, conductor, and musical director of many top Broadway musicals, including *Fanny*, *Wonderful Town*, *The Consul*, *L'il Abner*, and others. He is director of the Musical Theater Workshop of Broadcast Music, Inc., and executive director of musical theater development for Columbia Pictures Screen Gems.

Perhaps the most original and resourceful of Miss Baur's protégés was Faye Ferguson, of Ironton, Ohio, a pretty blonde pupil of Marcian Thalberg. In order to complete her musical education and launch her career as a concert pianist, Miss Ferguson incorporated herself under the laws of the State of Ohio as "Faye Ferguson, Incorporated," and sold shares of stock to her friends and other interested persons. One New York reporter, taking note of Miss Ferguson's unique approach to her problem, said: "Miss Ferguson . . . doesn't look at all like a corporation, but legally she is so many shares of preferred stock, just like the Standard Oil Company."

Another student in whom Miss Baur took a special interest was Robert Fulton Powell. In the summer of 1923, Mr. Powell came to the Conservatory from his native Mississippi to enroll in the voice department. Tall and slender, with a gentle smile and a courteous manner, he was liked by everyone. Miss Baur urged him to prepare for a career in opera, but Robert Powell was not interested in becoming an opera singer. His ambition was to enter the teaching profession, and to this end he directed his efforts. He was more than successful. His pupils, among whom was Metropolitan Opera star John Alexander, have invariably achieved distinction.

Robert Powell was one of the most popular and beloved teachers the Conservatory ever had. When he died suddenly in

41

August 1965, Henry S. Humphreys, music critic of the *Cincinnati Enquirer*, said of him: " 'Pupil of Robert Powell' after a singer's name is equivalent to the imprint 'Sterling' on silver."

Miss Baur followed with keen interest the career of another gifted young musician from the South, Jack M. Watson, of Dillon, South Carolina, who received his Bachelor of Music in 1930, majoring in vocal culture. She would be gratified to know that he is today the distinguished dean of the Cincinnati College-Conservatory of Music, and is well known as an author, singer, teacher, and administrator.

During his tenure of office at the College-Conservatory, Dr. Watson has made notable improvements in the curriculum and has effected many important innovations, including a radio-television department, which has prepared an impressive number of professionals in this field.

Bertha Baur was more or less formal in all her contacts, and was reserved, often to the point of coldness. It must be remembered that she took charge of the Conservatory at a time when women were not so strongly entrenched in business and the professions as they are today. Consequently, they were not always taken seriously, and Miss Baur, no doubt, assumed this reserved manner as a kind of armor. Leonard Liebling, editor-in-chief of the *New York Musical Courier*, recognizing Miss Baur's true worth in the professional world, wrote of her: "Miss Baur is a wonderful businesswoman and a rare idealist—a combination typically American and invariably successful."[1]

John Jacob Niles, celebrated ballad singer, composer, and arranger of folk music, is one of the Conservatory's most distinguished graduates. In an interview in the autumn of 1967, he recalled that most people thought of Miss Baur as proud and imperious. "I found just the reverse to be true," he said. "After I had been away for many years, I came back to the Conservatory to see her and, for reasons I could never tell, she simply engulfed me in her arms. 'You don't know how I have missed you,' she said, 'and now that you are successful, I am proud of you.' " Mr. Niles grew silent for a moment, seeming to be lost in thoughts of those far-off days. "I still remember her perfume," he mused. (It was old-fashioned *eau de violette* that she always wore.)

Occasionally there were lighter moments in which fleeting glimpses of the youthful Bertha, warm, genial, and vivacious, flashed through the stern facade that was her shield against an austere world. Such a moment is related by Miss Marionbelle Blocksom: "During the school year I conducted a class in ballroom dancing once a week in the gymnasium," Miss Blocksom said. "One evening dear Miss Bertha came up to watch the progress of the class, and a little later Mr. Thalberg also came in, no doubt to satisfy his curiosity. . . . When a lovely waltz was played and we were all dancing, Mr. Thalberg asked Miss Bertha to dance. As they waltzed around the room, all the young dancers stopped to watch them. Never have I seen such graceful dancing by two middle-aged, rather stout people. It was simply beautiful."

Being a person of strong convictions and positive opinions, Bertha Baur seldom hesitated to take a definite stand in any situation. She aroused intense feelings of animosity or adulation, and neither admirer not detractor could always tell exactly why. Yet it was these very traits—firm convictions, strong emotions and independence of thought—that made her a great leader. Whatever one's personal reaction to Bertha Baur, there was no middle-of-the-road response. It was impossible to remain neutral.

Alice Baur Hodges summed it up in one concise remark: "There were two schools of thought about Cousin Bertha. Either you loved her or you loathed her."

Miss Baur always found great satisfaction and relaxation in entertaining her friends. While her guest list usually included the elite of the music world, it was by no means limited to musicians. She counted among her friends interesting personalities from all walks of life: statesmen, writers, educators, artists, doctors, lawyers; the celebrated Cincinnati sculptor Clement Barnhorn, who designed the Clara Baur Memorial Fountain; the talented and vivacious actress Mary Boland; two eminent rabbis, Stephen S. Wise and Abba Hillel Silver; Bishop U. V. W. Darlington, whose daughter, Lyda Clarke, was a Conservatory graduate; King Albert and Queen Elizabeth of Belgium and their son, the Duke of Brabant (later King Leopold III), with whom she had lunch when Their Majesties visited the Queen City, and at least two presidents of the United States.

43

On one occasion, President and Mrs. Taft were guests of honor at one of Miss Baur's "little dinners," for which she was justly famous. The guests were to be entertained after dinner by the Conservatory string quartet. As they took their seats in the music room, Mr. Taft lowered his enormous bulk onto one of Miss Baur's fragile, antique chairs. Too frail to sustain his three-hundred-pound weight, the chair collapsed, the president falling to the floor. Neither Mr. Taft nor Miss Baur was in the least disconcerted. Miss Baur, with her usual aplomb, made a highly entertaining conversation piece of how the president of the United States fell at her feet.

Whatever zeal remained from Miss Baur's crowded schedule was used in tending her flowers. Gardening was the one hobby she permitted herself. She was often seen in animated conversation with Johann, her faithful, devoted gardener, directing the landscaping and planting of the Conservatory grounds. Johann, a thin, wiry little man with keen, intelligent eyes behind steel-rimmed spectacles, had come to Cincinnati from the village of Elsdorf on the Rhine, and was a wizard with the hoe and the spade. Under the gentle touch of his gnarled fingers, flowers blossomed in the most unpromising soil and in the most unlikely places. He could be seen almost any hour of the day spading, clipping, and pruning, with his duck-billed cap pulled over his eyes and smoking a huge pipe that looked more like a bass tuba.

Miss Baur had a great respect, amounting almost to reverence, for all green and growing things. She liked to feel the rich, warm soil in her hands and, when time permitted, tended the flower beds herself. Her pride and joy was a massive bed of tulips which she had planted between Shillito Hall and South Hall. In the springtime, when they flaunted their bright, variegated blossoms, the mass of color was pure drama. She was especially proud of her black tulips. The bulbs had been sent to her from Reütlingen, Germany, by her cousin, Dr. Julius Gayler.

Although Miss Baur had a sensitive appreciation for all nature, it was trees, from the flowering dogwood to the giant redwood, that held for her a special meaning. This love of trees was apparent in her daily speech as well as in her public utterances. In an address to the Class of 1915, Miss Baur appealed to the graduates to make the school grow like a tree. "It must become more beautiful, more useful," she said, "like the Cedars of Lebanon." To a later class, she said, "Make a friend of Mother Nature, cultivate an intimate acquaintance with her at first hand—she will richly repay you."

When it became necessary for Miss Baur to be absent from one of the annual alumni meetings, she sent a beautiful message to the Association, typical of her inmost feelings. "Greetings from a Colorado garden [the message read], beautiful with its laden fruit trees. To me, the Alumni Association is like such a tree, each year putting forth a new branch. May this year's bough bear abundant fruit and may the whole tree flourish for the security and prosperity of the Cincinnati Conservatory of Music."

In connection with trees, an amusing incident is told by the Baur family. Knowing Miss Baur's fondness for all trees, one of her friends, Mrs. E. L. Heine, sent to her on Christmas Day a rather large orange tree that she had grown in her own greenhouse. Not having sufficient space in President's House to accommodate a plant of this size, Miss Baur thought it would be a generous gesture to pass it on to Mrs. Mary Emery, who had a large conservatory. Mrs. Emery, in turn, thinking it would be an appropriate gift for Mrs. Heine, sent it to her. Before Christmas Day had come to a close, the orange tree had changed hands three times, coming to rest, finally, in its original greenhouse. Being blessed with an unfailing sense of humor, Miss Baur laughed with her two friends about the "traveling orange tree."

During the National Flower Show, which was held in Cincinnati in February, 1931, Miss Baur was accorded the honor of having a variety of snapdragon named for her. The "Bertha Baur Snapdragon," as it was called, was pale orchid in color, with long, slender leaves of dark green. It was developed in the nursery of Edward Schumann, a florist of Southgate, Kentucky, whose daughter, Peggy, was a Conservatory student. "Flowers and music are alike in many ways," Miss Baur said in accepting this honor. "They are both means of expressing beauty. Those who grow lovely flowers are in many ways like the musician who plays lovely music. In the same way, the creator of a new plant resembles a composer."

45

In the early spring Miss Baur watched the budding trees for the first signs of green tufts along the branches, and she watched for the first crocus with the eagerness of a child. Sometimes, when she was leaving her office at the end of the day, she would pause for a moment on the flagstones between Shillito Hall and President's House and look up into the leafy crowns of the sturdy old oaks, seeming to find renewal of spirit in their strength and beauty.

Chapter VIII

A HARROWING EXPERIENCE

The lamps are going out all over Europe; we
shall not see them lit again in our lifetime.
Edward, Viscount Grey of Fallodon, August 14, 1914, as the
lamplighters were turning off the lights in St. James Park.

In the summer of 1914, when Bertha Baur's regime was well
into its second year, she was beginning to show the strain of
unrelieved responsibility. Her family, concerned for her health,
urged her to go abroad for a well-earned rest. Late in July, after
the close of the summer school, she sailed for Europe. While she
was vacationing in St. Moritz, Austria declared war on Serbia.
She was staying in the same hotel where a score of Austrian
army officers were spending a few days' leave. On July 21, they
received orders to report at once for mobilization, and advised
Miss Baur to leave immediately, since there was little hope that
the war with Serbia would remain localized. She left on the
same train the officers took to Vienna. From Vienna she went
to Hamburg, where she had a reservation on the *S. S. Imperator*.
As she was preparing to go aboard, however, it was announced
that no passenger ships would be allowed to sail. To complete
an already distressing situation, her supply of gold was almost
exhausted, and paper money was unacceptable. She was unable
to obtain lodging because the hotels would not take her hundred-franc note. As she sat in the lobby of the hotel wondering
what to do, a German gentleman asked her if he could be of
assistance. She explained her predicament, showing him the
hundred-franc note. Without question he supplied her with the
equivalent in gold. Later, recalling the incident, Miss Baur said:
"I had never seen the man before, but his conduct was typical
of all foreigners I met after the trouble began.

"Transportation facilities were taxed beyond capacity," Miss
Baur said, "because of large numbers of soldiers being rushed to

the front. In one place I waited two hours and forty minutes to get my baggage." She also stated that she lent many of her garments to other women "who had lost all their baggage."

With all passenger sailings cancelled, Miss Baur pondered what was to be done. She decided that Holland would provide the best escape. From Hamburg she made her way to Rotterdam where the American Ambassador warned her that the whole country would soon be in a state of siege. She made the trip to Rotterdam with thirteen other passengers cramped into a small railway compartment originally intended to hold eight persons. Of this nightmare journey, she said, "We traveled all night, taking turns sitting down so that no one would be exhausted."

In Holland a week went by without any hope of securing passage to London. Finally, on the seventh day, it was learned that a boat would sail that night: a small steamer of the Holland-American line. As the ship left Rotterdam, they could hear the shelling of the big guns. The devastation of little Belgium had begun.

Of the voyage to London, Miss Baur stated: "The ship was small and the sea unusually rough, but I am a capital sailor and managed to avoid being seasick." She arrived in London in time to see the demonstration outside Buckingham Palace on the occasion of England's ultimatum to Germany. "I stood in the crowd," she said, "and watched King George, Queen Mary, and the Prince of Wales come out on the balcony and address the people. It was a scene of tremendous enthusiasm."

In London, Miss Baur found it almost impossible to get passage to America. "It was by the merest chance that I got my ticket," she said. "I bought it from an American I met on the street. His wife was ill and he was obliged to cancel their reservation." This reservation was on a small steamer, the *Corinthian*, which took fourteen days to reach Quebec. The *Corinthian* had been warned that German cruisers had been sighted along the coast. "To make the journey doubly dangerous," she recalled, "airplanes continually flew over our heads. Many passengers were afraid they belonged to Germany and would attack us. We were escorted far out into the Atlantic by a British squadron, which safely guided us over the mines laid for the enemy."

On a hot, sultry day late in August, Bertha Baur finally reached Cincinnati, after enduring three harrowing weeks in as many countries. She vowed she would "never again set foot on foreign soil." And, indeed, she never did.

Back in the United States, Miss Baur turned her boundless energy to the expansion of the school and to the improvement of the curriculum. At this time the study of opera was becoming increasingly important to American students. Each year aspiring young singers were going to Europe for operatic training and experience which they were unable to obtain in this country. Miss Baur was aware of this trend and felt that something should be done to halt it. "American schools of music must provide these facilities," she declared. "We must make it unnecessary for young artists to go abroad for this type of training and experience." It was characteristic of Bertha Baur that she "suited the action to the word," taking immediate steps to remedy this situation in her own school.

Although the Conservatory's voice department had previously presented scenes from the operas, Miss Baur felt that the time had now come to give students the opportunity of participating in full and complete operatic performances. Accordingly, in September 1916, she engaged a talented, dynamic young musician from Boston, Ralph Lyford, to take charge of the Conservatory opera department. His work with the San Carlo and Boston Opera companies and with the Pavlova Ballet was outstanding. His extraordinary ability and foresight were to have a far-reaching effect, not only in Cincinnati, but on the entire operatic scene.

Ralph Lyford was slight of stature, slender, and graceful, with dark, penetrating eyes and a somber expression. A shock of prematurely gray hair above a youthful face gave him an arresting appearance. He was intense and preoccupied, not given to small talk with his colleagues, and because of this seeming indifference he was seldom liked on first acquaintance. But those who worked with him and knew him well were fervent in their loyalty and devotion. He was greatly respected and admired for his sound musicianship, versatility, and accomplishment.

Mr. Lyford's first full-scale production as the Conservatory's director of opera was Offenbach's *Tales of Hoffmann*, complete with chorus, corps de ballet, and a fifty-piece orchestra, given at Emery Auditorium on March 17, 1917. Mr. Lyford took complete charge of the performance, and from the moment he lifted his baton, it was apparent that a master was at the helm. Among those who took part in this memorable production were Louis John Johnen, baritone, and Violet Summer, soprano, both Cincinnatians who eventually became members of the Summer Opera Assocation as well as teachers on the Conservatory faculty. The principals in the cast were: Manuel Valles, in the role of Hoffmann; Lucille Roberts as Julietta; Marie Hughes, in the part of Olympia, the mechanical doll; Flora Mischler as Antonia; and Mrs. William Evans as Nicklausse. Conservatory students and other promising young local singers assumed the secondary roles. With these complete operatic productions, Mr. Lyford placed the Conservatory far ahead of other schools in the presentation of grand opera as a strictly student endeavor.

The next important addition to the artist staff was Jean ten Have, well-known French violinist, whose superior musicianship and competence as a teacher had been widely recognized in his native France. As he was about to embark for the United States and Cincinnati, he wrote to Miss Baur with typical Gallic tongue-in-cheek. "I can speak the English language fairly well," he wrote, "and hope soon to be able to master the American dialect."

Mr. ten Have was a charming man, cosmopolitan in appearance, with a fine-featured, intelligent face and a neatly trimmed mustache; but what one noticed first were his long, tapering, artistic fingers. He was a man of few words, but his unfailing courtesy, kindness, and amiability soon endeared him to his associates as well as to his pupils.

On the occasion of his American debut, which occurred in Emery Auditorium in Cincinnati on October 20, 1916, the *New York Musical Courier* reported that "his American première left nothing to be desired in point of quality and color, refinement of expression, noble temperament and sympathetic virtuosity. His program was well outside the beaten path, and provided a number of welcome revivals and novelties. . . . George Leighton, of the Conservatory faculty, played Mr. ten

Have's accompaniments with taste and skill and shared in the honors of the evening."[1]

Shortly after his arrival in Cincinnati, Mr. ten Have became a member of the Cincinnati Symphony Orchestra, but resigned after a few years to devote his entire time to teaching. During his residence in Cincinnati, he served as French consul for a number of years.

Samuel Schindler, Cincinnati violinist and member of the Cincinnati Community Orchestra, was a pupil of Jean ten Have in the middle twenties. Recently, Mr. Schindler commented upon his former instructor. "He was a demanding teacher, but an inspiring one. During a lesson he frequently became so enthusiastic he would jump up and shout, *"Allons, allons,* let's go, let's go!' in a delightful mixture of French and English. And seizing his violin, he would play along with the pupil." Mr. Schindler also recalls that Mr. ten Have was "brilliant, suave, and literate," but at the same time "sort of down to earth. It was a privilege to study with a man of his stature."

The Misses Baur had been careful from the very beginning to select their faculty from widely divergent backgrounds, giving variety and balance to the curriculum, as well as imparting an international flavor to the campus. What was more important, students had the opportunity of instruction by master teachers without being obliged to go abroad. Miss Bertha did not, however, overlook capable American musicians who, up to this time, had been slow in receiving the recognition they deserved in their own country. In fact, the 1913-14 Conservatory catalog reveals that out of a faculty of fifty-five, more than half were Americans. At this time, the United States was still looking to Europe as the chief source of music, and Miss Baur had made frequent trips abroad in search of European artists who could bring added prestige to the school.

"Unfortunately, one must conjure with a name," Miss Baur was heard to remark in deploring the American custom of engaging European artists simply because they *were* Europeans. While abroad she attended concerts, operas, and other important musical events, interviewing potential teachers and "looking over the field." Today, this is the established recruitment procedure, not only among schools, but in sports and the professions. At the turn of the century it was not commonly practiced. Miss Baur should be considered, perhaps, as an early exponent of the "talent scout" system, as the term is currently used.

The first three years of Miss Baur's tenure of office came to an end with the dawn of the new year, 1916. The Conservatory had functioned like a finely-geared machine, and she had proved herself a worthy successor to her wise and gentle aunt. There had been no major crises, only the usual difficulties and problems inherent in administering the affairs of the school. Progress had been made in every department, with important revisions and innovations in the curriculum.

In the last months of the year, however, dark clouds appeared on the horizon, presaging an end to the halcyon days. Because of Germany's growing aggression, it had become evident that America would not long be able to maintain a policy of neutrality in World War I. Then, on March 18, when German submarines sank without warning three American merchant ships, the die was cast. On April 6, Woodrow Wilson, then president of the United States, drove sadly through a soft, spring rain to the Capitol and called upon the Congress to make a declaration of war against the aggressor.

Chapter IX

"A QUAINT LITTLE LADY"

Music my rampart, and my only one.
Edna St. Vincent Millay, *On Hearing a Symphony of Beethoven*

If one is to understand the aims and objectives of the Cincinnati Conservatory of Music and the principles upon which it was founded, it is necessary to know something of its history and that of the young German girl, Fräulein Clara Baur, whose idealism, vision, and perseverance led her to establish this great American school of music.

Historians have written numerous accounts of the founding of the Conservatory, its subsequent development and its influence in the field of music education, but scant material is found about the young woman who created this institution. We find almost nothing prior to 1857, and the facts pertaining to her childhood and adolescence are so scarce as to make it almost impossible to reconstruct those early years. Clara Baur kept no diary and wrote no memoirs. There is scarcely a shred of her correspondence to be found, and the persons now living who knew her are so few that we can know very little about her thoughts and feelings. Apparently, she took no thought of how future generations would appraise her life, nor was she concerned with the measure by which historians would assess her deeds. The only memorial she sought was in the lives of the young people whom she prepared for useful careers and sent out into the world to take their proper places in society.

Existing records in the possession of the Baur family reveal that Clara Baur was born in Stuttgart, Germany, on December 10, 1835, the daughter of the Reverend George Ludwig Baur and Maria Fredericka (Finke) Baur. Her mother died when she was born.

From her earliest years Clara Baur's all-consuming pass` ｣ seems to have been music. She attended the Stuttgart Music

School, devoting herself to the study of piano and theory. In a letter from her cousin, Herr Karl Baur, of Stuttgart (dated December 10, 1968), he writes: "It is certain that her piano teachers were Messrs. Dr. Sigmund Lebert and Ludwig Stark." Herr Baur also states that "today's College of Music dates back to the 'Music School' founded by Sigmund Lebert and Immanuel Faisst. . . . Only in the year 1865 did it become the 'Conservatory' and in 1897 the 'Royal Conservatory.' "

Clara Baur was a tiny, fragile-looking person, barely five feet tall, and her thick, curly hair above a serene brow was auburn. "A quaint little lady," someone said of her, "who was so kind and gentle that one could scarcely realize her greatness."[1] Pianist H. Ray Staater, who taught at the Conservatory under Miss Clara's direction, recently said of her: "Since she was outwardly shy and reserved, one was surprised to find that underneath this gentle manner was a will of iron. She was often able to have her own way simply because of her patience and perseverance.

A portrait of Miss Clara, painted in oils by the American artist Louis Schwebel in 1884, shows a serious face with deep-set eyes and a square, determined jaw, softened by the generous lines of her mouth.

Alice Baur Hodges recalls that Miss Clara's strength and endurance belied the smallness of her frame. "She always gave the impression of needing protection," Mrs. Hodges said, "but this was totally false."

Shortly after finishing her studies at the Stuttgart Music School, Clara Baur came to Cincinnati for an extended visit to her brother, Theodor. She was persuaded to give private piano lessons, using the drawing room of her brother's home on Milton Street as a studio. She also took advantage of the opportunity of studying vocal culture with Madame Caroline Rivé, one of America's outstanding vocal teachers of the time.

Mrs. Kenneth Lawwill (Katherine Baur) remembers hearing her father, the late George A. Baur, say that Clara had a brief career as a concert pianist in Germany. She gave it up, however, in favor of teaching because she found the public appearances "too nerve-wracking."

"While Clara Baur's career began as a private teacher," Miss

Bertha stated on one occasion, "always uppermost in her mind was the dream of establishing a music school to be modeled after the great conservatories of Europe."

When Clara Baur decided that Cincinnati was the most advantageous location for her proposed school of music, and when her plans had been formulated, she returned to Germany and re-entered her alma mater to study the methods of that famous old school. This was around the year 1858. Some time later (the exact date is not known) she went to Paris for further study. In his history, *Cincinnati: The Queen City*, Charles Frederic Goss states that she "continued her work in vocal art with Madame Moroncelli, a famous opera star, and with Madame Winter-Weber, one of the prima donnas of the Paris Grand Opera."[2] At the conclusion of her study in Paris, Clara returned to Cincinnati, feeling that she was now ready to embark upon the great undertaking for which she had prepared herself.

It has been established beyond question that 1867 was the year that the Cincinnati Conservatory of Music was founded. There is one dissenting voice. Charles Frederic Goss places the years as 1869. However, the Cincinnati Historical Society has in its possession the school's first catalog: a slender, modest little publication of a dozen pages, giving the exact opening date—December 2, 1867.

There are also conflicting statements by historians as to Clara Baur's age at this time. It has been generally accepted that she was twenty-two years of age when she returned to Cincinnati and opened her studio on West Seventh Street. George Mortimer Roe gives her age as twenty-two,[3] as does Lewis A. Leonard.[4] Goss, again dissenting, places her age at sixteen.[5] The Baur genealogy, revealing that Clara Baur was born in 1835, proves all three of these historians in error. She was thirty-two years of age when she founded the Cincinnati Conservatory of Music. Mr. George Baur recalled that Miss Clara had "always been secretive about her age," that she went to great lengths to conceal the exact date of her birth, seeming to derive a whimsical amusement in checkmating the inquisitive. Her age was her own secret which she guarded throughout life—and beyond—for her birth date was not noted even on her gravestone.

Why did this diminutive, blue-eyed German girl wish so fervently to establish a school of music in the United States? Why did she leave family and friends to cast her lot among strangers in a foreign land? Why did she choose Cincinnati instead of New York? Or Cleveland? No one seems to know for certain. It has been suggested that perhaps she realized Cincinnati's central location would provide easy access from all parts of the United States and, since her plans included a boarding department, this would seem to be the most logical choice.

During her first visit to the Queen City, Clara had surely taken notice of the numerous well-organized musical groups that had made this frontier village the undisputed center of music culture in the Midwest. Music was taught in the public schools and, in fact, the life of the entire community was permeated with music. Among the oldest and most ambitious of these were the Orpheus Society (1817), the Handel and Haydn Society (1819), and the German-American Cecilia Society, formed and directed by the famous Herr Ritter.[6]

America's first *Saengerfest* was held in Cincinnati in 1849; by 1857, when a special building was erected for the occasion, nearly two thousand singers made up the chorus. That same year the *Maennerchor* and the Philharmonic Society got under way.[7]

At this period in the history of Cincinnati, Germans formed a large percentage of its population. This, no doubt, influenced Clara's choice of location, as she must have realized that wherever Germans congregated there would be music.

Another deciding factor, aside from the simple wish to be near her brother, may have been the lack of competition. There were few, if any, schools of music in the United States, and none in the Midwest. America still looked to the Old World as the source of music, but Clara Baur saw no reason why talent could not be developed here as well as in Europe. This was the task she set for herself. She had no capital, and her knowledge of the English language was limited, but she determined, with hard work and perseverance, to overcome these twin obstacles. Little did she dream that she would change the whole concept of music education in her adopted country and by so doing, become famous on both sides of the Atlantic.

Before continuing her journey to the Queen City, Clara Baur

stopped for a visit in New York City, and was warmly welcomed into a select coterie of musicians. New Yorkers looked upon their city as the center of culture in the United States, the Mecca of visiting European artists. They eagerly exhibited its cultural advantages to the visitor from Germany: the French Theatre, the German Opera House, and the New York Academy of Music, celebrated for its distinguished operatic performances, boasting the most famous singers of the time. It is certain that she would have attended some of these performances, followed by a gala supper at Delmonico's and a moonlight drive in a hansom cab through Central Park.

It is an interesting coincidence that Theodore Thomas was at this time playing in the violin section of the orchestra at the Academy of Music. While it is unlikely that he and Miss Clara had met during her visit in New York, their paths converged a few years later in a most significant manner. While Miss Clara was launching her fledgling Conservatory, Theodore Thomas became the conductor of the newly-formed Cincinnati May Festival Chorus, in which a large number of Miss Clara's students participated. With her friend Mrs. Bellamy Storer, Miss Clara worked tirelessly to assist Mr. Thomas in making the festival a success. In 1878, Mr. Thomas was appointed as the first director of the Cincinnati College of Music. Thus, these two talented young musicians, both born in Germany only two months apart, were responsible in a large measure for laying the foundation of Cincinnati's illustrious musical tradition.

During her stay in New York City, Clara Baur's friends tried to persuade her to stay there. They urged upon her the advantages of a large metropolis to a musician of her attainments. "Why leave the cultural atmosphere of the East for a crude frontier settlement in the far West? Why not establish your school here?" they asked. New Yorkers no doubt considered Ohio an unbroken wilderness and Cincinnati a backwoods outpost with Indian encampments on the outskirts of the city.

Colonel James H. Mapleson, considered the most authoritative impresario in Europe, upon hearing of Miss Clara's plans, advised her to open her school of music in New York City, "the only logical place for such a venture." Nevertheless, Clara Baur was not tempted to remain in New York. She had chosen

Cincinnati as the location best suited for her school and she would not be persuaded to change her mind.

On a bright, frosty morning in early autumn, she left New York on the last lap of her journey. Crossing the Alleghenies by stagecoach, she boarded a steamer at Pittsburgh and came down the Ohio River to the Queen City. As she stepped ashore on that autumn day in 1867, she had no hint of the obstacles to be met and overcome before that "bright, bright day" when all her dreams would come true.

Chapter X
"BEHOLD THE CONSERVATORY OF THE FUTURE"

Without Music, life would be a mistake.
Nietzsche

Clara Baur found that many changes had taken place in the Queen City during her absence in Europe. The War Between the States had come to an end; the suspension bridge across the Ohio River, a marvel of engineering, had been completed and opened to traffic, and Pike's Opera House, destroyed by fire the previous year, was being replaced by a large concert hall. The residential section of the city was moving out "on the hills" where elegant homes were being built.

German immigrants, who now formed a large portion of Cincinnati's population, had settled on the northern end of Vine Street and in the "elbow" of the canal. They had built homes, churches, business houses, and the inevitable beer gardens so dear to the German heart. On West Seventh Street, close by this colony of her countrymen, Clara Baur rented a few rooms from the "Misses Nourse's School for Young Ladies" and opened the Cincinnati Conservatory of Music, "the first Conservatory west of Boston, the Boston Conservatory preceding it by only a short time."[1] With great care and discrimination she chose top-ranking musicians for her faculty, each a specialist in his own field, setting a high standard of instruction that has never been lowered.

The Conservatory's first faculty, announced in its initial bulletin (1868-69),[2] was composed of Miss Clara Baur, directress; Mr. H. G. Andrès, director of the faculty; Madame Caroline Rivé; Signora Giannini; Professors G. A. Schmitt, L. S. Du Sape, Theodore Holle, Leo Kofler, J. de Ricqles, J. Blum, and Louis Schwebel.

The curriculum was ample and diversified, consisting of piano, organ, violin, violoncello, band and orchestral instruments, cultivation of the voice, all theoretical subjects, German, Spanish, and Italian.

In 1870, Michael Brand, a distinguished Cincinnati musician, was employed by Miss Clara to teach violoncello. Mr. Brand, whose concert band included the finest musicians in the city, was a member of Cincinnati's most proficient musical family. His forty-piece orchestra was the nucleus around which the Cincinnati Symphony Orchestra was formed in 1895.

In the Conservatory's third annual catalog (1870-71), eight additional teachers were added to the roster. Included in this number was Miss Emma Heckle, prominent Cincinnati singer, whose triumphant career spanned more than fifty years. At this time, a children's department was opened, the first regularly established department for juveniles in the city.[3]

Although the school had prospered and its reputation had become widespread, the path was constantly beset by obstacles. In addition to the "Money Panic" of 1873, which placed a great strain on Miss Clara's financial resources, there was the impossible task of renting or leasing a suitable building large enough to accommodate the expanding enrollment. For the first time, a small, dark cloud of doubt appeared on the horizon. Had this indeed been God's plan for her life? Or had she allowed her own desires and ambitions to obscure His real purpose?

It was during this crucial period that Miss Clara had a vision: a vision so vivid, so compelling, that to doubt its reality would be to deny the the evidence of her senses.

Late one afternoon of a cold winter's day, Miss Clara stood at the window of her studio watching the last rays of a fiery sunset spread across the western hills. Suddenly, in the afterglow, she saw a castle-like building, crowned by a large belfry, taking shape against the translucent sky, seeming to be sketched by an unseen hand. Then, she saw a finger point dramatically to the finished drawing and she distinctly heard a voice say, "Behold the Conservatory of the future."

Was this a divine revelation, or merely the illusion of a tired mind? Miss Helen May Curtis had not a moment's doubt that it was an inspired omen. "Miss Clara was deeply spiritual," Miss Curtis said. "She seemed to have intuitive powers beyond the scope of the five senses." There were others, however, who were skeptical of the "vision," believing that Miss Clara had mistaken illusion for reality. Yet even the skeptical did not question her sincerity.

Miss Clara herself was so convinced of the reality of her vision that when she saw the Shillito mansion she recognized her "castle in the clouds." When the concert hall was built adjacent to Shillito Hall, it was crowned by a belfry, an exact replica of the one she had seen in the sky on that winter's day thirty years before.

With the coming to power of the Hayes administration, the effects of the 1873 depression subsided. The financial situation was stabilized and banks that had failed during the Grant administration were re-opened. The tide of prosperity was mounting, and with this new affluence came a renewed interest in the fine arts and the leisure in which to pursue them. Once again, Miss Clara found it imperative to seek larger quarters. With the help of her brother, Theodor, she found a large, four-story building at the corner of Eighth and Vine Streets that would be suitable for her needs.[4] This became the Conservatory's second home and "boarding students were admitted for the first time in the history of American schools of music."[5] At this time Miss Clara was reponsible for another "first." Believing that continuity of study is essential to the mastery of music, she inaugurated the summer school, "the first regular summer music school in the United States."[6]

The Conservatory's boarding department proved successful beyond Miss Clara's fondest hopes, especially with patrons from the South. With the end of Reconstruction, prosperity was returning and education, so tragically interrupted during the War Between the States, was again of paramount concern. The Conservatory, with its central location, its cultural advantages, and homelike atmosphere, fulfilled a need for a "home away from home" for young ladies from a distance.

By this time, Bertha Baur was assuming an increasingly important role in the administration of the school. She was listed in the catalog as "secretary and preceptress." With the move to Vine Street, Miss Clara's dream for her school was becoming a reality. Such a high degree of excellence had been attained that its reputation extended far beyond the confines of the United

States, and students were being enrolled from abroad. The *New York Musical Courier* noted that "not only is the boarding department filled with students from abroad, but all of the boarding places in the neighborhood are supplied with Conservatory students."

"The fame of this unique little woman," said one historian, "and the school she had created, was eventually carried back to Europe by visiting artists. Such interest was aroused that when Lilli Lehmann came to Cincinnati to sing in the May Festival she visited the Conservatory to 'see for herself' if rumors had been exaggerated."[7]

About this time, the Conservatory had another famous visitor, equally enthusiastic about its quality of instruction: Madame Adelina Patti, the celebrated coloratura, came to the Queen City under the auspices of the London impresario, Colonel James H. Mapleson, to sing in the Opera Festival. She was the guest of honor at a reception given by the Misses Baur and presented them with a signed photograph as a memento of her visit.

In 1897, Madame Etelka Gerster, the great Hungarian soprano, made a concert tour of the United States. Her appearance in Cincinnati was the musical highlight of the season, and Miss Clara was in the audience with her nieces. The *Cincinnati Times-Star* noted that "Miss Clara wore a gown of black satin garnished with jet, Miss Bertha was gowned in black crepe, and Miss Wanda wore pale blue chiffon."

During the engagement, Madame Gerster was entertained at the Conservatory and, like Madame Patti, presented Miss Clara with an autographed photograph in remembrance of the occasion. In 1877 Madame Gerster had married Dr. Carlo Gardini, director of the Italian Opera Company, and was now the mother of a small daughter. She had been engaged by Colonel Mapleson to make the tour, but she had made it a condition that she be allowed to bring her baby with her. Years later, this "baby," named Berta, married the eminent orchestra conductor Fritz Reiner. During his tenure as conductor of the Cincinnati Symphony Orchestra, 1923-31, Madame Reiner became a member of the voice faculty of the Conservatory.

In 1884, due to the large number of boarding students, Miss

Rev. A. J. Nast, Miss Pennell, Marie Nast (age 8 years), "Grandpa" Nast, Miss Carrie Clark, Miss Annie Howard, Miss Clara Baur, Miss Hayes (?), William A. Gamble, son of the co-founder of the Procter & Gamble Company, Cincinnati, Ohio. Taken at Lakeside, Ohio, 1888

Courtesy of Mrs. Marie Nast Wherry

Clara and Miss Bertha found that they needed more dormitory space. Accordingly, they leased a larger building located at 140 Broadway. However, when the lease expired, they decided not to renew it. Because of the steadily increasing commerce on the Ohio River, Broadway was becoming a noisy, congested thoroughfare. The boat landing was only a short distance from the school, and the discordant sounds of the river traffic could be distinctly heard at the Conservatory. Speaking of those days, Miss Bertha remembered that "one could hear the roaring of the lions and the trumpeting of the elephants as the circuses were brought ashore." Clearly this was not the place for a music school. Once again they looked for a new location.

In the spring of 1892, due largely to Miss Bertha's efforts, the Conservatory's fourth home was found: a spacious, red-brick mansion situated at Fouth and Lawrence Streets, the original site of Fort Washington. It had been the home of General Lytle, but in later years was owned by Washington McLean, the colorful editor of the *Cincinnati Enquirer*. The staircase leading to the second floor was of such exquisite design that guests invariably exclaimed, "What a beautiful staircase for a bride to descend!" So far as is known, it was not used for such a romantic purpose during the Conservatory's occupancy; however, the possibilities of this excellent feature were not overlooked. During the annual Christmas carol service, white-robed choristers carrying lighted tapers descended the stairs singing the traditional carols. In this beautiful setting the Conservatory grew and flourished for eleven years.

It was while the Conservatory occupied the McLean mansion that another of Miss Clara's nieces became affiliated with the school: Miss Bertha's sister, Wanda Constance Baur.[8] Miss Annie Howard said of her, "She was so gay, charming, and vivacious she was like a breath of spring." Herbert Silbersack recalls that she was a "gentle, lovely little lady, not austere like her sister Bertha."

Bertha and Wanda were the *alpha* and *omega* of the Emil Baur children, being separated by almost eighteen years. As the youngest of the family, Wanda was pampered and petted by her indulgent parents and alternately teased and spoiled by her adoring brothers.

Wanda had come to the Conservatory to attend the University of Cincinnati, but soon found herself involved in the activities of the school. "If tempers flared," Alice Baur Hodges remembers, "it was Wanda who poured oil on the troubled waters."

Before the year 1894 was very far advanced, fate struck a shattering blow to the Baur family. Professor Emil Baur died at his home in Ann Arbor. Because of failing health and the dissolution of *Ora Labora*, life became intolerable for this sensitive, warmhearted man, who had asked only for the privilege of helping the needy and the destitute of his adopted country. He thought he had failed, but had he lived a few years more, he would have seen that his noble experiment was the means of bringing prosperity and stability to that part of Michgan.

To leaf through the Conservatory's early catalogs, yellowed and musty with age, is like raising the curtain on a Victorian play. Rules and regulations, consistent with that era, would seem quaint and droll to the Conservatory student of today. The faded records reveal an age in which the conduct of young ladies was definitely prescribed and rigidly enforced. Voices were to be kept soft and low at all times, in what Miss Clara called the "princess pitch." If things became too noisy, she would speak to the culprits with gentle reproof. "Girls, girls, remember princess pitch and fairy footsteps."

The catalog stated plainly that parents should make their traveling arrangements so that "pupils will not arrive on Sunday." Students were always met at the railroad station upon their arrival in Cincinnati and accompanied to the Conservatory by a chaperone. Miss Helen Moore Smith, a young lady from Philadelphia, acted as a "train chaperone" for four years. In an interview with the *Cincinnati Post*, October 30, 1914, Miss Smith said that she had met more than three thousand girls at the train and, during all those years, had missed only three.

There was positively no practicing on Sunday. Out of respect for the Sabbath, all musical instruments were to be kept closed. Voices were not to be raised in song. "Quiet hour" was strictly observed.

The catalog also stated: "The rules and regulations which refer to students' conscientious employment of time, and their correct deportment within and without the school-room, will likewise be but in conformity with the desires of every young lady whose mind is duly impressed with the responsibility of her position in society."

In addition to the printed regulations in the catalog, Miss Clara had some unwritten rules of her own—very strict ones—as to how a young lady should conduct herself. "No dressing on the street, not even putting on gloves." Another private rule directed the young ladies "when strolling on the campus to stay within forty feet of the gates."

In the early catalogs, pupils were listed alphabetically, but *separately*—"ladies" first, "gentlemen" second—a fine distinction, but wholly in keeping with this chivalrous age. The roster of students included the daughters and sons of Cincinnati's pioneer families, names that have been prominent for many years in the cultural, professional, religious, and civic life of the city: Groesbeck, Graeter, Kahn, Ludlow, McLean, Perin, Sattler, and Shillito, among many others.

Miss Clara believed that cultivation of the social graces was absolutely essential to a student's overall education. The 1896 catalog lists a course in "deportment for young ladies." This class was taught by a Miss Eckert, but was personally supervised by Miss Clara herself. It was well known, however, that she knew very little about the culinary arts. On one occasion,while a Thanksgiving feast was being prepared, Miss Clara asked the cook if she could be of any help. She was told that she could "baste the turkey." She excused herself for a moment saying that she would be back shortly. When she returned to the kitchen, she was armed with a large needle, a thimble, and a spool of thread, and announced that she was ready to "baste the turkey."

During Miss Clara's lifetime, it was customary to have morning prayers and daily Scripture reading. Constance Baur Morse described the scene: "At the close of the breakfast hour, Aunt Clara would come from her private dining room . . . ring a bell for silence, read the Bible verses, then all would join in the Lord's prayer, after which the students were dismissed."

Speaking of those days, Ray Staater commented: "Sometimes Miss Clara would dispense with the usual form of worship and, in her own words, offer the morning prayer. You have never heard such prayers. Straight from the heart of this wonderful woman, they were an inspiration to everyone."

Storms might swirl about Clara Baur, yet, like the eye of the hurricane, she remained constant, pursuing her calm and ordered way, serene and confident in her faith.

Chapter XI

"TO THE PRAISE OF GOD AND THE STUDY OF MUSIC"

The aim and final reason of all music
should be nothing else but the glory of
God and the refreshment of the spirit.
Johann Sebastian Bach (1685-1750)

In 1902 the Conservatory was destined to make its final move. The years from 1884 to 1900 had been a turbulent period in the Queen City. The economy was recovering from the Depression of 1873 and money was plentiful. The city was "wide open" and honest citizens were outraged by graft, crime, and corruption. Vine Street, once a respected business section, had become a noisy, brawling midway. A red-light district openly flourished; gambling was tolerated. The infamous "Courthouse Riot" had shocked the city. Taking the law into their own hands, an angry mob had stormed the jail and burned the courthouse in an attempt to lynch a certain prisoner. "When the two-day mêlée had ended, fifty-six persons lay dead and some three hundred wounded."[1] A month preceding the Courthouse Riot, Cincinnati experienced the most disastrous flood in its history. The entire business section was inundated and thousands were left homeless in the wake of its devastation. The Misses Baur were convinced that the time had come to move away from the dangers and distractions of the downtown district.

From the very first, Miss Clara's plans had included the purchase of a permanent site for her school. Miss Bertha, who was now in complete charge of the business management, urged her aunt to look for a suitable location. About this time, the Shillito mansion was offered for sale. Built in 1867 in the suburb of Mt. Auburn, at Highland Avenue, Burnet Avenue, and Oak Street, it was formerly the home of the John Shillito family. The finest craftsmen in America had been employed to make it one of the most palatial homes in the Ohio Valley. With its many spacious rooms, its handsome appointments, and beautifully landscaped grounds, it was an ideal setting for a music school. Remembering her vision and believing she had been divinely led, Miss Clara hastened to purchase the magnificent property for the Conservatory's permanent home.

The *Cincinnati Commercial Tribune* of September 2, 1902, described the Conservatory's new site in the "decorated" literary style of the day:

> Situated on a gentle summit overlooking the whole valley at a distance of only twelve minutes from the center of the great city below, palpitating with the noise and tumult of its strenuous life . . . this fair home of Music rises stately and serene from out a grove of forest trees which shades without concealing the classic symmetry of the building.

Now followed a decade of untroubled years, sadly to be the last decade of Miss Clara's life. These were tranquil days, peaceful and unhurried. The nation was prospering. No war clouds darkened the sky and no "isms" threatened to disrupt the national unity. Cincinnati's own William Howard Taft became president of the United States during this time. It was the "Age of Elegance," an era of lavish hospitality, imported lace, rustling silks and feathered fans. Americans were prosperous and content. There was leisure for the cultivation of the arts, and music-loving Cincinnatians made the most of it. Prominent families sent their children to "Miss Baur's Conservatory," as it was called, to be educated musically.

The Misses Baur—Clara, Bertha, and Wanda—numbered among their friends the greats of the music world: Paderewski, Schumann-Heink, Melba, Nordica, Companini, Caruso—the list is endless. The Conservatory's beautiful drawing room was the gathering place for visiting artists. Dr. John A. Hoffmann remembered "many inspiring evenings" spent in the company of these famous musicians. Outside, the ground might be covered with snow and the thermometer hovering around zero, but in the Conservatory drawing room was warmth, hospitality, and witty conversation. Here, before a blazing log fire in the huge wood-burning fireplace, an impromptu concert or *Saengerfest* might take place: the world's greatest artists making music for the sheer joy of it.

Caruso called the Conservatory his "little home" and never failed to visit when he was in or near Cincinnati. He had known Tirindelli in their native Italy when both were impoverished young musicians struggling to gain recognition in the capitals of Europe. Years later, when they met in the United States, they were both famous: Tirindelli as a violinist and composer, Caruso as the world's most renowned tenor, known everywhere as the "voice of gold." When they met in the Conservatory drawing room, as they frequently did, they would reminisce for hours, making light of their early hardships.

Caruso was gay and fun-loving, with a bubbling sense of humor and a penchant for playing practical jokes. He was a gifted cartoonist, and liked to dash off caricatures of his friends and present them at the most inopportune moments. Tirindelli was often the target for his jokes. The April, 1910 issue of *Sharps and Flats* published a reproduction of a caricature which Caruso had drawn of himself and Tirindelli, signed by the great tenor himself.

Another favorite visitor to the Conservatory was the fabulous Madame Schumann-Heink, who never failed to call on the Misses Baur whenever she appeared in Cincinnati. Paderewski was often a guest for dinner or an informal luncheon.

Very few persons were privileged to really know Miss Clara Baur. She was not without a certain formality of manner, and insisted that the proprieties be observed at all times. Dr. Hoffmann spoke of her as "kind, considerate and gentle, but always rather aloof."

"While it is true that she was exacting of her pupils and her associates," Miss Annie Howard said, "it is also true that she was exacting of herself. She believed that the greater the talent, the greater the responsibility for its use. For one to waste or neglect his God-given talent was to her a 'cardinal sin.' "

Clara Baur has been called "intrepid" by two historians. At least one has called her "foolhardy." An incident which proves her right to either or both of these titles occurred while the Conservatory was still on Broadway. It is cherished by the Baur family and repeated with a great deal of enjoyment.

70

One evening in early summer, Miss Clara suddenly realized that the dinner hour was drawing near, but no sounds were coming from the dining room. This was unusual. Normally, one heard the "clink" of silverware and the subdued murmur of voices as the evening meal was being prepared, but on this particular day there was absolute silence. Miss Clara went to investigate. She found the dining room empty of servants, but looming in the doorway was a huge, shaggy lion, switching his tail and snarling in a menacing manner. Miss Clara did not hesitate. With all the strength of her less than one hundred pounds, she shoved the intruder out of the door and slammed it in his face. Then she calmly went about the business of rounding up the cooks and waiters who had fled the scene and locked themselves in the pantry. Later, it was found that a circus had come to town that day and, during the unloading of the animals, one of the lions had escaped, finding its way to the back entrance of the Conservatory kitchen.[2]

During the Conservatory's seventieth anniversary celebration in April, 1937, five of Miss Clara's former pupils were in attendance, each of whom was more than sixty years of age: Mrs. Nellie Dietterich McFee, Mrs. Alice Teasdale Fisher, Miss Hattie Levy, and Miss Frances Moses (who served on the Conservatory voice faculty for more than thirty years), all of Cincinnati, and Mrs. E. H. Hart, of Meridian, Mississippi.

Mrs. Hart, director of the Meridian School of Music and one of the Conservatory's most illustrious graduates, remembered Miss Clara as a "gracious figure in her lovely, soft black dress, with a bit of lace at the throat, tripping on French heels up and down the stairways."

Mrs. McFee, who was eighty years old at the time of the celebration, recalled that Miss Clara would give her a "gentle poke" in the back to make her "stand up straight." Said Mrs. McFee. "She taught me much more than music."

The year before Miss Clara's death, a new dormitory for girls was completed in time for the opening of the fall term. On the day of the dedication, her strength seemed to transcend the frailties of her seventy-six years. As she cast the first spadeful of earth about the cornerstone, her face was radiant with joy and the pride of accomplishment. In a ringing voice she dedicated

71

the new building to "the praise of God and the study of music."

The pathway from the small studio on West Seventh Street to the magnificent campus with its imposing array of buildings had sometimes taken strange and devious turnings. For more than forty years Miss Clara had held fast to her dream. Its eventual fulfillment is a testimony to the vision, patience, determination, and good judgment of this "unique little woman" who had created this great institution. She had cast a small stone into the water. The ripples had reached to distant shores and encompassed countless lives.

During the one-hundredth anniversary celebration of the founding of the Cincinnati Conservatory of Music, Mrs. Morse, who was Miss Clara's great-niece, related the circumstances of her death. "I was with her minutes before she died," Mrs. Morse said. "We had just finished making out her class cards for the day, and I had returned to my room. I had hardly reached my door when someone called me to come quickly, that Aunt Clara had fallen. She was lying on the floor outside the office door. She was carried into a studio across the hall and a doctor was summoned, but it was too late. I am sure she must have died when she fell. Aunt Clara had always said that she wanted to 'die in harness,' and this last wish was granted.''

Miss Millie Muckerheide, Miss Bertha's personal maid and faithful companion, recalls that Miss Clara "lay in her casket in the drawing room of Shillito Hall, surrounded by hundreds of floral offerings, dressed in a black satin gown with a touch of white lace at her throat. In her hands was a sheaf of lilies of the valley, a token of love from her domestic staff. Each one of us added a blossom until the bouquet was complete."

Members of the teaching staff, among whom were Albert Berne, Ray Staater, and Hugo Sederberg, watched beside her casket while grieving friends, professional colleagues, and fellow citizens came to pay their last respects to this "unique little woman" whose entire life had been dedicated to the teaching of music.

Clara Baur was laid to rest in Spring Grove Cemetery, in Cincinnati, on Friday morning, December 21, 1912, while the sun shone intermittently through thin gray clouds. The trees had long ago shed their leaves and a light, powdery snow lay

Clement J. Barnhorn 1913

The Clara Baur Memorial Fountain, the work of Clement J. Barnhorn, erected on the campus in 1913

along the bare branches. The casket was borne to the graveside by Miss Clara's nephews, Theodor Baur, Jr. and George A. Baur, both of Cincinnati, Doctors Emil and Adelbert Baur, of Chicago, and two of her dearest friends, Robert E. Sattler, a Cincinnati Physician, and Frederic Shailer Evans. The burial service was conducted by the Reverend Jacob Kapp, pastor of the Elm Street Lutheran Church, where Clara Baur had been a regular communicant since coming to Cincinnati.

I am the resurrection and the life.... The familiar, comforting words were spoken by the Reverend Kapp as the flower-covered casket was lowered into the frozen earth. A chill wind whispered through the evergreens and rustled the dry leaves. *He that believeth in me, though he were dead, yet shall he live....*

Clara Baur's song of life had ended, but its stirring melody would echo through the years in the hearts of those whose lives she had touched. With her going, the door was closing upon an era. The quiet charm, the gracious, leisurely ways of "Miss Baur's Conservatory," would soon be only a memory.

"No one can fully estimate the power and influence of such a life," wrote the Reverend John H. McKenzie, rector of the Home School in Cincinnati. "Thousands have been inspired by her character. They have felt the power and inspiration of her life. . . . The world is all the richer because Miss Clara Baur lived and worked."[3]

74

Chapter XII

OPERA AND RADIO

There is sweet music here that
  softer falls
Than petals from blown roses on
  the grass. . . .
    Alfred, Lord Tennyson, "The Lotus-Eaters"

The history of opera in Cincinnati has been told many times. It is sketched here briefly only to bring into proper focus Bertha Baur's place in this artistic endeavor, and to disclose her little-known efforts to promote opera in the Queen City.

During the first two years of Miss Baur's tenure as director of the Conservatory, scenes from the operas had been presented by students in the opera department. In 1916, Tirindelli, Ralph Lyford, and Miss Minnie Tracey had prepared and staged scenes from *Romeo and Juliet, L'Africaine* and *Mefistofele*. The next year the first complete opera was undertaken, *The Tales of Hoffmann*, given at Emery Auditorium, with full orchestra, chorus, and ballet.

In May, 1917, Leonard Liebling, editor-in-chief of the *New York Musical Courier*, came to Cincinnati especially to attend the Conservatory's presentation of *La Habanera*. Mr. Liebling expressed his approval of this performance in an editorial which he wrote for the magazine upon his return to New York. "Ralph Lyford, instructor of opera and of theory and composition at the Cincinnati Conservatory of Music, who had coached the singers and staged the opera, also conducted it. Owing to his careful training and inspiring instruction, the participants in the performance went through it with a confidence and surety rarely witnessed in amateurs, which made the whole presentation assume quite a professional character."[1]

Previous attempts had been made to produce opera in Cincinnati—mostly in the light opera category—but it was the

75

Conservatory opera department, under the direction of Ralph Lyford, that laid the foundation of what came to be the Summer Opera Association.

Ever since he had joined the Conservatory faculty, Mr. Lyford had cherished the dream of giving to the city of Cincinnati its own resident opera company. Now, after two seasons of successful student productions, he felt that the time had come for the launching of such an enterprise. Realizing that the greatest problem facing the opera students was gaining the necessary experience to begin an operatic career, Miss Baur enthusiastically endorsed Mr. Lyford's idea of a permanent opera company in Cincinnati. She would be in the unique position of being able to render invaluable service to the company by supplying much-needed talent, at the same time providing talented students with the opportunity for practical stage experience. In fact, she has been credited with being the "mysterious person" who gave Ralph Lyford the idea in the first place. This, however, is only conjecture.

The Cincinnati Zoological Gardens, with their abundant shade and beautiful lake, had become a center of outdoor entertainment for Cincinnatians. There were band concerts, dining and dancing in the clubhouse, and an ice show. This, it had been decided, was the ideal setting for the new opera company. Arrangements were made for a season of six weeks. The year was 1920.

Sunday evening, June 27, was warm and fragrant, with a starlit sky: a perfect summer night for the opening performance of this ambitious group. The pavilion was thronged with music lovers who had come to see the curtain rise on the Queen City's newest musical organization, an event whose far-reaching impact on the music world was not contemplated even by the most perceptive.

As the orchestra took its place in the pit, the house lights began to dim, voices were hushed, and late-comers hurried quietly to their seats. Expectancy and promise hung in the air: a moment of magic, mystery, and anticipation. Even the ducks on the lake were silent, the lions ceased their restless whuffling, and the Zoo's aged, wizened elephant, "Old Lil," forbore to trumpet in the June twilight.

Promptly on the stroke of eight, Ralph Lyford, immaculate in white linen, made his way from the wings to the podium. This quiet, soft-spoken young man, whose zeal and perseverance had made this evening possible, gravely acknowledged the tumultuous applause that greeted his appearance. The signal was given, the orchestra began the familiar and melodious overture to Flotow's *Martha*, and the Cincinnati Summer Opera was on its way.

In the cast on this historic evening was John Jacob Niles, now an internationally recognized composer, arranger, and singer of folk songs—known as the "grand old man of American folk music." Mr. Niles has many nostalgic and amusing recollections of those first performances.

"Ralph Lyford did it!" he said in a 1967 interview. Then he added, with a twinkle in his keen, blue eyes, "You see, Ralph had to have someone to back him up in the pinches, sing extra parts, hold the prompter's book, and what have you. So, I painted scenery, managed the lighting, and helped other members of the cast with their makeup—'all things to all men,' you might say. Once I even substituted for an ailing soprano in *Hansel and Gretel*. Just at curtain time, the Dew Fairy, her face a faint greenish hue, fled from the stage, muttering: 'I'm going to be sick.' " Mr. Niles did not hesitate. In less time than it takes the Wicked Witch to invoke her magic spell, he had donned the costume of the Dew Fairy and was ready to assume the role.

Then, there was his recollection of one performance of *The Barber of Seville*. "As stage manager," he said, "I used a stiff froth of egg whites as lather in the shaving scene. One night, for some reason, this chore was entrusted to a stagehand named Charlie. Instead of the usual egg white, Charlie added a note of realism. He whipped up a heavy lather of soap which Figaro used much too freely on Dr. Bartolo's face, most of the lather going into poor Bartolo's eyes. After the performance, Bartolo (played by the young Italian basso, Paola Quintana), with a murderous gleam in his eye, went looking for Charlie. 'Where "Sharlie," where "Sharlie?" ' he demanded of everyone he met. But 'Sharlie' had long since disappeared down a side street."

The "Zoo Opera," as it is familiarly known, seems to have

been beset by more than its share of on-stage accidents, some amusing, some distressing. None of the other mishaps, however, can compare with a performance of *Carmen* in which a member of the male chorus lost his pants. A wave of unsuppressed laughter swept through the audience while the unfortunate chorister hastily retrieved the lost garment. Yet, so well disciplined was the cast that not one single note was missed. Fausto Cleva, who was on the podium that night, seemed completely oblivious to the incident.

In the early days of the Summer Opera, the choruses, the ensembles, and the *corps de ballet* were made up of students from the Conservatory, the College of Music, and private studios in the city. This was an ideal arrangement, affording ambitious young artists the rare opportunity of actual stage experience while working closely with the professionals who assumed the leading roles. These principals were recruited from the Metropolitan, the Ravinia, the San Carlo opera companies and the Chicago Civic Opera, and included such well-known singers as Henriette Wakefield, Edith de Lys, Melvena Passmore, Salvatore Sciarretti, Robert Maitland, and Marie Valle.

Mr. Lyford drew his own sketches for most of the stage settings and had them built locally, since there were no scenic supply houses in Cincinnati. In many instances the scenery was hastily assembled and none too sturdily built, the paint barely dry before it was used. Any unnecessary vibration could have caused a major disaster.

The costumes for the choruses were frequently left to the ingenuity and resourcefulness of the individual, since there was seldom time or money to rent them. Consequently, they were sometimes inappropriate, sometimes novel, and occasionally startling, but these were minor imperfections. If the costumes were less than authentic and the scenery a bit sleazy, the performance itself was truly professional. Ralph Lyford would tolerate nothing less.

Among the Cincinnatians who joined the opera cast the second season (1921) was Pearl Besuner, soprano. Miss Besuner remembers vividly her first performance with the company. "The opera was *Martha*," she recalls. "My costume was made of heavy velvet and stiff brocaded satin, with long, tight-fitting

78

sleeves and a high neck. The temperature in Cincinnati that night was in the nineties, and the dressing rooms below the stage had very little ventilation. We all but roasted. This was an inconvenience in retrospect only," Miss Besuner said. "We were young, eager, and ambitious, willing to give 'our all' for Art." After a successful engagement with the San Carlo Company, Miss Besuner went on to New York to become the first Cincinnati Conservatory of Music student to be accepted by the Metropolitan Opera Company, paving the way for other Conservatory students who have since been so honored.

Ralph Lyford successfully managed and conducted the Cincinnati Summer Opera for five consecutive seasons. Yet, when negotiations got under way for the selection of personnel for the next season, dissension arose between the management and certain other groups. Finally, the rift became so serious that Mr. Lyford, already ill from overwork, felt it was in the best interests of the company for him to resign.

This turn of events was a stunning blow to Ralph Lyford. He had worked ceaselessly and unselfishly to promote his fledgling company, and his inability to continue as its director hurt him deeply. Shortly after his resignation, he took a long leave of absence from his teaching duties at the Conservatory and his position as associate conductor of the Cincinnati Symphony. He visited England, Switzerland, and France and, during this time, was invited to conduct the Geneva Opera Company and the Paris Grand Opera. A long list of honors attest to the appreciation and recognition of Mr. Lyford's work. Among his many awards was the David Bispham Silver Medal given by the American Opera Society for his opera, *Castle Agrazant*, which was also selected as one of the three best American operas submitted in a nationwide contest.

On September 3, 1927, death cut short the career of this versatile young musician. He had returned to Cincinnati only the day before to make final arrangements for assuming his duties as conductor of the St. Louis Municipal Opera for the coming season. Ralph Lyford had been on the Conservatory faculty for twelve years, and there was shock and grief among his colleagues when his death was announced. "He produced opera at the Conservatory magnificently," Miss Baur stated to the press. "He was highly thought of both as a musician and as a personality." One of his close friends stated that "Ralph Lyford died of a broken heart. He could not bear to see someone else reap the rewards of his labors."

As a continuing result of Mr. Lyford's efforts, the Cincinnati Conservatory has been privileged to give to the operatic world some of its brightest stars: Susanne Fisher, Pearl Besuner, Grace Divine, Everett Marshall, John Alexander and, in recent years, Julian Patrick and ballerina Suzanne Farrell.

After the death of Ralph Lyford, Miss Baur was faced with the task of finding someone to take his place as head of the opera department and musical director of the Conservatory Orchestra. She appealed to her old friend, Paderewski, who warmly recommended Alexander von Kriesler, a native of Russia, distinguished on the continent as a conductor and opera coach.

Mr. von Kreisler, born to wealth and affluence in Petrograd, had been destined for a career as an officer in the Imperial Guard, or a post in the diplomatic service. He went abroad for his early education, later returning to Petrograd to enter the university for the study of law. But young von Kreisler's ruling passion was music, for which he had shown unusual talent. In addition to the study of law, he enrolled at the Imperial Conservatory, devoting as much time as possible to music. His chief interests lay in the fields of opera, composing, and conducting. When the revolution broke out, his knowledge of music became, literally, a lifesaver for the von Kreisler family. Although his services were requisitioned by the Bolshevik government, he stated that he was "glad to be a musician." It assured him of a livelihood when others in his class were "thrown into absolute destitution."

In the autumn of 1928, Mr. von Kreisler arrived in the United States from Riga where he had been conducting the Riga Symphony Orchestra. In the meantime, he had married a famous dramatic actress, Maria Kirsanova, whom Miss Baur employed as director of acting and *mise en scène* of the opera department. Madame Kirsanova was a charming woman, with a queenly grace and a hauntingly beautiful face. The joint efforts of her husband and herself resulted in productions that were fresh and unhackneyed, giving distinction to the department. Their presentations consisted mainly of Russian operas— Tschaikowsky's *Eugen Onegin* and *Picque Dame*, Rimsky-Korsakov's *The Czar's Bride*, and other operas which, up to this time, had not been widely performed in Cincinnati.

During the time Mr. von Kreisler taught at the Conservatory, he owned a German police dog named Jimmy, whose dislike for Brahms was legendary. He attended every rehearsal, waiting quietly and patiently to accompany his master home—that is, until a Brahms number came up for rehearsal. Then he would get up, give Mr. von Kreisler a reproachful look, and stalk out. His dislike for Brahms remains an unsolved mystery.

While Ralph Lyford was establishing the Zoo Opera in Cincinnati, Powell Crosley, Jr. was experimenting with the field of radio broadcasting, a new and exciting medium in which Miss Baur also took an active interest. Mr. Crosley's first broadcasts originated in the living room of his home. Later, the equipment was installed in the Crosley factory on Arlington Street where, in March, 1922, the first message was transmitted under the call letters WLW.

Powell Crosley was one of the giants of this growing industry. He owned and controlled the first radio broadcasting station in the Queen City: The Crosley Broadcasting Company. As the decade progressed, however, other broadcasting stations were established in greater Cincinnati: WSAI, sponsored by the U.S. Playing Card Company, opened a studio in 1923, WKRC in 1925; and WCKY in 1929.

Because of radio's unprecedented growth and public acceptance, there was an overwhelming demand for talent and material to fill the ever-increasing hours of broadcasting time. Miss Baur urged the Conservatory students to take advantage of appearing before the microphones as a means of gaining experience in actual public performance. In most instances, they gave their time and talent without compensation.

The Conservatory had a delightful custom of providing the artists for Sunday afternoon musicales held in the homes of Miss Baur's personal friends and other Cincinnati music lovers. Jane Froman, one of Mr. Beddoe's outstanding pupils, was soloist on one of these occasions when Mrs. Charles P. Taft was hostess. Mr. Powell was present and was so impressed with Miss Froman's beautiful contralto voice that he invited her to become a member of the WLW artist staff. She remained with the Crosley Station for several years, then went to New York and began a radio series which established her as a major entertainer. She had a successful career in radio and musical theatre and as soloist with Paul Whiteman's orchestra. Other gifted young Conservatory students who delighted radio listeners in those early days were Wilma and Nadelle Schupping (the "Singing Schupping Sisters"), Violet Summer, Iliah Clarke, Harry Nolte, and Ben Alley. As early as 1923 WLW experimented with scenes from the operas. *Romeo and Juliet* was presented with a cast of Conservatory students, including Lucy de Young, Kathryn Reese, Clifford Cunard, Howard Fuldner and Lawrence Wilson. The regular Saturday morning broadcasts of the Conservatory Symphony Orchestra, under the direction of Alexander von Kreisler, were perhaps the school's most significant contribution to radio broadcasting. Introduced on the air by the *Romanze* from Mozart's *Eine Kleine Nachtmusik*, these programs were eagerly awaited by music lovers all over the country. One former student wrote to Miss Baur: "I almost commit *hara-kiri* if anything interferes with my Saturday morning radio program from the Conservatory. . . . I have heard so many fine things." Katherine (Baur) Lawwill, the daughter of the late George A. Baur and a cousin of Miss Bertha Baur, played in the cello section of this group of fine young musicians.

Miss Baur was delighted that these programs were the means of bringing pleasure to so many people. She treasured the letters and expressions of appreciation she received from listeners from all walks of life. Yet, being an astute businesswoman, she could not have been unaware of the advertising value of these broadcasts as they brought the Conservatory into thousands of homes from coast to coast.

Chapter XIII

THE WAR YEARS

Cry 'Havoc, and let slip the dogs of war. . . .
Shakespeare, *Julius Caesar*, Act III, Scene 1

"The Spirit of Democracy glorifies and exalts the American nation. It was born of the blood of martyrs whose names illuminate the pages of American history," said Miss Bertha Baur at the 1918 Alumni Association banquet. "The youth of our country heard the call and, as one voice, came the answer: 'Here am I, send me!' Forty-two of our Conservatory boys took up the cry and in clarion tones their voices rang out: 'Here am I, send me!' "

The war with Germany was a bitter blow to Miss Baur. The roots of the Baur family had been, since the fifteenth century, deep in the history of Germany. Miss Clara's sister, Mrs. Louise Mayer, still lived in Reütlingen, and communication with her and other members of the family was cut off. Miss Clara had been a great admirer of Kaiser Wilhelm II, and in one issue of the school magazine had quoted his "Rules of Life" as a model for the students.

"The war really troubled Miss Baur," John Jacob Niles recalled. "On one occasion she said to me: 'You can't imagine how I suffered for my family: kindly, honest burghers who never harmed anyone, and now they are being blamed for the cruelties of the army and the havoc they have wrought in Belgium.' "

On the Conservatory faculty were a number of German-born teachers who, understandably, were racked by a deep division of loyalty. Theodor Bohlmann, who was born near Halberstadt in the Hartz Mountains, had come to America as a young man. He had been a prominent member of the Conservatory faculty and a respected citizen of Cincinnati for more than twenty years. Wilhelm Kraupner, highly regarded as a pianist, com-

83

poser, and teacher on the artist staff, was also a native of Germany.

Many other Conservatory teachers who had received musical training in this ancient and beautiful land were deeply distressed by the turn of events. John Hoffmann, Louis Saverne, Albert Berne, Peter Froehlich, and George Leighton were among those who had taken postgraduate work in Berlin, Leipzig, and Hamburg. Dr. Edgar Stillman-Kelley, who had been a student at the Stuttgart Conservatory where Miss Clara Baur had received her early training, dedicated his *Macbeth* music to "His Imperial Majesty Wilhelm II" in remembrance of the hospitality he had enjoyed during his long residence in Berlin.

The involvement of the United States in the war with Germany brought a sudden and drastic change to the atmosphere of the Conservatory campus. Red Cross rallies, bond drives, and rousing speeches had inflamed young hearts with patriotic fervor; martial music, flying banners, and blaring bugles had stirred the blood and set the feet to marching. Bach, Beethoven, and Brahms were temporarily shelved in favor of such exciting war songs as "Over There," "My Buddy," "There's a Long, Long Trail." The excitement was contagious. Everyone rushed to "do his bit." Miss Baur watched with a heavy heart, yet proudly, as one by one her "boys" left the Conservatory to "make the world safe for democracy." The October, 1918 issue of *Sharps and Flats* listed forty-five Conservatory men in the service of their country, among whom were such talented young artists as Dwight Anderson, Chalmers Clifton, Ray Staater, Lloyd Miller, and Irving Miller. Lloyd Miller wrote entertainingly to his teacher, Mr. Evans, of his duties as assistant to the chief surgeon in an evacuation hospital in France. "We hear the guns and see the fire at night," he stated, "besides experiencing night raids made on our own hospital."

Throughout the war years Miss Baur made a great effort to insure the continuation of the Conservatory's full educational program. Nevertheless, she felt that the students should not be insulated from the impact of America's role in the war. Students and teachers who remained on the campus were encouraged to give as much time as possible to the Red Cross and other patriotic groups. Miss Baur had for many years been an active member of the American Red Cross, contributing generously to its causes. During the war she redoubled her efforts, employing every means at her disposal to assist this organization in its important work.

By this time hundreds of American soldiers were already in France. Literally dozens of civilian organizations were engaged in the war effort, and Miss Baur was constantly called upon to furnish musical programs for these various groups. It would be impossible to determine the number of civic and religious agencies that were indebted to Miss Baur, at least in part, for the success of their wartime projects. One such organization was the Cincinnati and Hamilton County Council of National Defense, for which she provided a chorus of one hundred Conservatory girls to take part in the celebration of the French National Holiday in July, 1918. In December of that year, the Conservatory Symphony Orchestra braved one of the worst blizzards in the city's history to give a concert for the Cincinnati chapter of the Italian Red Cross. For arranging this program Miss Baur was given a standing ovation and a letter in which the council expressed its "sincere thanks and sense of obligation for this courtesy."

Years later, Robert Powell (who was a veteran of World War I), commented on Miss Baur's ingenuity and her ability to get things done. "If Miss Bertha had been Field Marshal instead of von Hindenburg," he said, "Germany would have won the war." Mr. Powell greatly admired Miss Baur, and he made the remark facetiously, but the concept is not so farfetched. Anything Bertha Baur wished to do, she could have done. She was brilliant, farsighted, and determined. Above all else, she was a great personality. She could have successfully ruled an empire or won a war.

Although the Baur family was deeply concerned for the safety and well-being of their kinsfolk in Germany, they remained the most loyal of American citizens, sending their sons into the conflict on the side of the Allies. Samuel Baur, son of Theodor Baur, Jr., of the First National Bank, volunteered his services in the early days of the war and was sent overseas as a member of the ordnance department. Another cousin of Miss

Baur's, Corporal Harry Froehlich, of Cincinnati, gave his life for his country. He was killed in action in the Meuse-Argonne Sector just twenty minutes before the news of the armistice reached the front lines. In a letter to the bereaved family, Captain John Emerson said: "I was quite near him and saw him fall—as a hero should—with his face toward the foe. . . . He gave his all for a principle which he thought to be right and just."

At the outset of World War I many Cincinnatians of German descent were sympathetic to the cause of Germany. A large number of older citizens who had emigrated from Germany still had close family ties there. Most of them spoke very little English, but their children and grandchildren were bilingual.

A few Cincinnatians openly declared their allegiance to *Der Vaterland*, but those who were rash enough to do so soon had cause to regret it. Dr. Ernst Kunwald, conductor of the Cincinnati Symphony Orchestra, found to his sorrow that his imprudent remarks would not be tolerated by the American government. Shortly after war was declared, he stated publicly from the podium in Music Hall that he expected to remain a loyal subject of Germany. After leading the orchestra in the playing of "The Star-Spangled Banner" (which was the customary opening for all symphony concerts), he turned to the audience and said, "But, of course, my heart is on the other side." There was a shocked silence; some hissed, others left the hall. Feelings were running high and, for this indiscreet pronouncement, Dr. Kunwald was arrested, hustled off to prison and interned as an enemy alien for the duration of the conflict.

In this highly-charged, emotional atmosphere, almost anyone with a German name was suspect. Theodor Bohlmann and his lovely wife were harrassed by scathing remarks, threatening telephone calls, false accusations, and rumors of their alleged connection with a supposedly subversive group known as the "People's Council of America." Finally, they felt obliged to make public denial through the medium of the press. In a signed statement appearing in the *Cincinnati Enquirer*, October 8, 1917, Mr. and Mrs. Bohlmann declared: "We expect to die as loyal Americans, true to the cause of our country."

It would seem unreasonable that the Bohlmanns should have been suspected of subversion and made the subject of unwarranted suspicion and harrassment. A few years before the war, Mr. Bohlmann had married one of his pupils, the beautiful and talented Miss Susan Monarch, from Owensboro, Kentucky, a member of one of the oldest and most distinguished families in that part of the state. Mr. Bohlmann was a beloved and trusted member of the Conservatory faculty and highly respected in Cincinnati. Of his loyalty to his adopted country there could be no question. As a concert pianist, Theodor Bohlmann was widely known and acclaimed throughout the Midwest. Short, rotund, and good-humored, his audiences "took him to their hearts" from the moment he walked on stage. In a small college town in Kansas, the students cheered his performance with tumultuous enthusiasm. After the concert, they unhitched the horses from the carriage which was to convey him to the railroad station (this was in the "horse and buggy" era), and pulled the vehicle themselves, with Mr. Bohlmann triumphantly seated inside the carriage.

By some miracle, Bertha Baur remained calm and unperturbed in the midst of the turmoil and prejudice caused by the war. In spite of the disruption, however, she did not relax her efforts to provide qualified teachers to fill the vacancies left by those who had entered the armed services, nor did she neglect the program of expansion to which she had committed herself.

Fronting on Highland Avenue near the corner of Auburn Avenue, and adjacent to the Conservatory on the south, was a handsome, spacious, red-brick house, formerly the home of the late Charles Durrell. In May 1918, Miss Baur learned that this property was being offered for sale. She promptly bought it and, eventually, it came to be known as South Hall.

In the autumn of that same year, a young Irish tenor, Thomas James Kelly, was added to the voice faculty. Now, the Conservatory had two men of the same name—Dr. Edgar Stillman-Kelley and Dr. Thomas Kelly—although they spelled their surnames differently. Dr. Thomas James Kelly would have been distressed if an "e" had been used in the last syllable of his name, while Dr. Edgar Stillman-Kelley would have been equally disturbed if it had been omitted from his. For purposes of differentiation, the students soon referred to these interesting men as "Dr. Edgar Stillman" and "Dr. Thomas James." Each of these musicians, in his own special way, has left an indelible imprint on the history of the Conservatory of Music and on the cultural life of the Queen City.

Dr. Thomas James Kelly had come to the United States from the Province of Ulster where he was born and educated. Not only was he a thorough musician, he was also gifted with a keen mind, a ready wit, and a charm of manner that could be attributed only to his Irish ancestry. Cincinnatians were quick to recognize his skill as a lecturer and narrator, and soon he had more requests for speaking engagements than his crowded schedule would permit him to accept. He will long be remembered for his interpretations of the Cincinnati Symphony's concerts for children. With his imaginative narration, the compositions of the masters became real to his youthful listeners. They were enchanted with the music of *Hansel and Gretel*, the *Dance of the Sugar Plum Fairy*, and other pieces so dear to the hearts of the very young. In 1930, Dr. Kelly was appointed director of the Orpheus Club, one of the oldest and most important musical organizations in the city, a post he held for many years.

In the summer of 1918, Miss Baur engaged the master violinist, Eugène Ysaÿe, to conduct a master class for advanced violin students at the Conservatory's summer session. The internationally famous violinist and conductor had fled his native Belgium when it was overrun by the invading German armies. After a harrowing journey across the country to the coast, he escaped to London in a small open fishing vessel, carrying with him his most precious possession, his Guarnerius violin, but little else. He remained for a while in England, then went to New York where he maintained his professional headquarters until he was called to Cincinnati to become conductor of the Cincinnati Symphony Orchestra. Here he found that Emil Heermann, the son of his old friend Hugo Heermann, was concertmaster of the orchestra. The post of conductor had become vacant due to the unfortunate incident which resulted in the dismissal of Ernst Kunwald. Ysaÿe entered upon his new duties in October, at the same time continuing to teach a master class at the Conservatory.

Mr. Arthur C. Bowen, well-known cellist who played in the Cincinnati Symphony Orchestra under Ysaÿe's leadership, stated that "Ysaÿe's master violin class at the Conservatory attracted widespread attention. Violinists came from great distances to take advantage of the unusual opportunity of receiving instruction from this world-famous musician."

Ysaÿe's quiet dignity and dark, brooding intensity gave him the appearance of taciturnity, but this was not the case. He has been described by those who knew him best as a "big-hearted gentleman, a loyal friend to young aspirants, and at times the jolliest of good fellows."

At the time of his appointment as conductor of the Cincinnati Symphony, Ysaÿe brought with him an outstanding young musician to occupy the desk of first cellist with the orchestra. His name was Karl Kirksmith. Before coming to Cincinnati he had been solo cellist with the Minneapolis (Minnesota) Symphony Orchestra, as well as a member of the New York Philharmonic, the Sinsheimer String Quartette, and the Dzerwonsky String Quartette. Miss Baur was fortunate to secure his services as a member of the Conservatory teaching staff.

In the midst of the hardships, sacrifices, and deprivations of the war, Miss Baur was called upon to endure a sorrow which made all else seem trivial. On December 24, 1917, her mother died suddenly of a heart attack. Bertha Herzer Baur divided her time between her daughters in Cincinnati and her sons in Chicago. She had come to Cincinnati for an extended visit when her death occurred.

Mrs. Baur was small, cheerful, and lively. Her voice was low and musical and, although she had lived in the United States for all but ten of her seventy-six years, she still spoke with a slight accent which people found charming. Mrs. Morse remembers with affection this tiny, red-haired Saxon beauty who was her grandmother. "We loved her very much," Mrs. Morse said. "She was so kind to my mother and taught her many things about German cooking. I still remember the wonderful dumplings she used to make for us when we were children."

Miss Millie Muckerheide also had fond memories of Mrs. Baur. "She was very devout," Miss Muckerheide recalled. "It was my duty to read to her every night from the Episcopal prayer book. After prayers she would often reminisce about the days of her childhood in Saxony, remembering the strict rules in those days. No cooking was allowed on the Sabbath. All food had to be prepared on Saturday and only warmed on Sunday."

Bertha Herzer Baur was buried in Bethlehem Cemetery in Ann Arbor, Michigan, the day after Christmas. Her body was placed beside that of her beloved husband, Emil, and close by were the three small graves of their children, Henry, Augusta, and Clara, whose lives had ended almost before they had begun.

Chapter XIV

"A WOMAN OF FINE PRESENCE"

For manners are not idle, but the fruit of
loyal nature and of noble mind.
Alfred, Lord Tennyson, *The Idylls of the King*

November 11, 1918. Germany had surrendered and the war
was over. When it became known that hostilities had ended,
Conservatory students abandoned, for the moment, the "Art
Divine." Pianos were closed, harps were hastily covered, and
classes went unattended while everyone joined the hysterical
throng that converged on Fountain Square to celebrate the
armistice. Sirens blew, horns honked, bands blared and there was
impromptu dancing in the streets. Factory whistles were shrill
and insistent, contrasting sharply with the solemn tolling of
church bells. The Kaiser was burned in effigy. The boys were
coming home. The world was "safe for democracy."

After the feverish activities of the war had subsided, Miss
Baur turned her attention to the long-delayed program of expansion, which had been postponed because of the war. Her
first step was the purchase of the house next door to South
Hall, an exact duplicate, to be used for additional studios and
for her private residence. It soon became known as President's
House. These identical houses had an interesting history. They
were built by identical twin brothers, Charles and Joseph
Durrell, shoe wholesalers of Cincinnati, who had molded their
lives along exact lines, even being married on the same day in a
double ceremony, and living side by side in identical houses.

The next year Miss Baur bought another valuable property: a
large, three-story stone building across the street from the twin
houses and facing on Auburn Avenue. It was named Auburn
Hall and was used as a dormitory. A carriage house in the rear
of the lot was converted into an experimental theatre to be used
as a workshop by the Conservatory's dramatic club, The Garret

Players. The stage, workrooms, and studios of this unique "little theatre" were housed in the garret portion of the building, hence the names "The Garret Theatre" and "The Garret Players." Under the direction of Miss Margaret Lovisa Spaulding, this ambitious group presented many original plays as well as standard repertory.

The *Musical Leader* of May 26, 1919, noted that "Miss Bertha Baur, of the great Cincinnati Conservatory of Music . . . spent a short time in New York where, between visiting friends, she looked over the musical field." It was during this visit to New York City that Miss Baur engaged Dan Beddoe, internationally known Welsh tenor, as a member of the Conservatory artist faculty. Upon her return to Cincinnati she announced that he would arrive in the Queen City in September to enter upon his duties at the beginning of the 1919-20 fall semester.

Dan Beddoe was at the height of his artistic maturity, already beloved of Cincinnati audiences, having been acclaimed as tenor soloist at three May Festivals: 1908, 1910, and 1914. Cincinnati music lovers received the news of his Conservatory appointment with pride and satisfaction: a happy reunion between artist and audience. Mr. John A. Hoffmann observed that Mr. Beddoe's voice was a "God-given gift." Said Mr. Hoffmann: "Nothing seems to interfere with his flawless production. I have seen him eat an enormous meal, smoke a big, black cigar, then get up and sing like an angel."

During his long residence in Cincinnati, Mr. Beddoe was tenor soloist at the Seventh Presbyterian Church in Hyde Park where he sang to overflow crowds every Sunday morning for ten months of the year. He had appeared repeatedly with the Cincinnati Symphony Orchestra under the batons of Van der Stucken, Kunwald, and Stokowski before coming to Cincinnati to make his permanent home.

In the summer of 1919, Miss Baur announced that two famous pianists would soon join the teaching staff: Marguerite Melville Liszniewska, known as the "Poetess of the Piano," and Monsieur Jean Verd, distinguished French virtuoso.

Madame Liszniewska, an exponent of Leschetizky (and his associate in Vienna), had made an enviable reputation in Europe as a composer as well as a pianist. Her pianoforte quintet caused one Viennese critic to remark: "If a woman can create a serious chamber music work like this . . . we can only advise her male competitors to look quickly for another trade."

Madame Liszniewska was born Marguerite Melville in New York City. When her extraordinary talent became evident, she was sent to Berlin to study with the eminent pedagogue Dr. Ernst Jedliczka. So impressed was he by his gifted young pupil that he called her his "little Mozart."

Marguerite Melville Liszniewska was a charming woman with a grace of manner and a dignity of bearing that gave her a commanding stage presence. She had a flair for the dramatic and anything she undertook was accomplished with taste and imagination. She even selected her dogs from an uncommon breed. Anyone who knew "Madame" will remember the pair of perfectly matched, snow-white borzois that frequently accompanied her on her walks.

Dr. Karol Liszniewski, also a gifted pianist, accepted Miss Baur's invitation to join his wife as a member of the Conservatory artist faculty.

Monsieur Verd was counted among the leading young Parisian pianists. He was the holder of the *premier prix* of the Paris Conservatoire, and the *Prix de Rome*, and was also a member of the *Societé des Concerts du Conservatoire*. M. Verd had become well known in this country through his appearances with the eminent cellist Pablo Casals and the Danish Soprana Povla Frijsh. The *Cincinnati Enquirer* observed that his "coming to Cincinnati is of significant moment."

With the program of expansion progressing so rapidly, the crescendo of work began to mount, and Miss Baur realized she could no longer carry the burden of management without assistance. Consequently, she looked about for someone who would be qualified as general manager. She was fortunate in securing the services of a brilliant young man from the East, Burnet C. Tuthill. At thirty-one, he was a successful business executive and also an accomplished musician, the perfect combination for the position Miss Baur had to offer. Handsome, alert, and knowledgeable, Mr. Tuthill entered upon his new duties with zeal and enthusiasm equalled only by his efficiency and resourcefulness. When he assumed the office of general manager on July 1, 1922, *Sharps and Flats* observed: "Mr. Tuthill's successful business experience and his musical efficiency doubles his value."

Mr. Tuthill's notable service to music and musicians makes him worthy of more than passing mention. He received his education at Columbia University, where he was awarded both the Bachelor of Arts and the Master of Arts degrees. He had always manifested a keen interest in all forms of music, but showed special aptitude in the fields of ensemble. His instrument was the clarinet, which he played with skill and artistry. While he was general manager of the Conservatory, Mr. Tuthill found time to organize the National Association of Schools of Music, which was established to help solve problems of accreditation between Conservatories and Colleges. He served as secretary of this organization for thirty-five years, beginning with the first meeting in 1924. During this time he directed the girls' glee club at the University of Cincinnati as well as the Conservatory choral group, and taught ensemble at the National High School Orchestra's summer camp at Interlochen, Michigan.

In recent years, Mr. Tuthill has devoted a great deal of time to composing, resulting in an impressive number of compositions ranging from orchestral works to songs. He believes his best compositions are *Bethlehem* and *Come Seven*, for orchestra, and *Big River*, for women's chorus and orchestra. He is now retired after serving as professor of music at Southwestern University, in Memphis, Tennessee, director of the Memphis College of Music, and conductor of the Memphis Symphony Orchestra, which he organized in 1938.

As the school expanded, the need increased for teachers in all departments. In 1924, Miss Baur announced the apointment of Parvin Titus as a teacher of organ. Dr. Titus is one of the country's truly great organists. He received his training in Paris with the French master Marcel Dupré and in New York with the Belgian organist Gaston-Marie Déthier. Shortly after his arrival in Cincinnati, he accepted the position as organist and choirmaster of Christ Church, a post which he filled with distinction for thirty-five years. He also served as organist for the Cincinnati Symphony Orchestra and the May Festival for twenty-five years. Now, as organist and choirmaster of Christ Church in Glendale and a teacher of organ at the College-Conservatory of Music, Dr. Titus remains active in the musical life of the city.

Other significant apointments followed; Madame Karin Dayas, internationally known pianist; Robert Perutz, violinist, and Mieczyslaw Munz, Polish pianist, who came to fill the vacancy caused by the serious illness of Monsieur Verd.

Driven from Poland by political strife and internal wars, Mr. Munz arrived in America with little but his press notices to introduce him into the musical life of this country. Although he had a well-established reputation in Europe, Mr. Munz was unknown to the American public. He was able, however, to arrange for a series of recitals in Aeolian Hall in New York City. His reception was overwhelming and his success assured.

In the summer of 1926, Madame Dayas was added to the artist faculty. She came to the United States with her husband, August Soendlin, a well-known violinist and violist, whom she married in Berlin in 1916. Mr. Soendlin played for many years in the viola section of the Cincinnati Symphony Orchestra. The artistry of these two fine musicians was a source of great pleasure to Cincinnati music lovers.

Karin Dayas was noted not only for her colossal repertoire, which she played with superb musicianship, but she was also recognized as a superior teacher. She served on the faculty of Cincinnati's College-Conservatory of Music for forty-five years and in 1964 received the University's "Dolly" Cohen Award for excellence in teaching. Madame Dayas died suddenly on March 4, 1971.

One of the most popular and beloved of the younger teachers of the mid-twenties was Thomie Prewett Williams, who was graduated from the Conservatory in 1922. Miss Baur was impressed by the performance of this talented young pianist from California and persuaded her to remain as a member of the Conservatory teaching staff. During her residence in Cincinnati, she was pianist for the Heermann Trio, a notable chamber music group organized by Walter Heermann and his brother, Emil, members of the famous Cincinnati musical Heermann family. When Mrs. Williams died in 1932, the *Cincinnati Enquirer* said, "Her life was so full and complete in its service to others as to wear itself out after only a brief span."

Under Miss Baur's effective leadership, the Conservatory now consisted of a complex of five magnificent buildings, a faculty of more than seventy-five and the largest student body in its history. Because of her incredible achievement, Bertha Baur was attracting attention as one of the outstanding business and professional women in the country. The New York *Musical Leader* stated in an editorial: "Miss Baur is a woman of fine presence, a superb mentality, and her refinement and culture are in themselves guarantees for the class of work that emanates from the Cincinnati Conservatory of Music. A woman of this quality at the helm of musical institution is a strong argument in favor of the fact that America is the place to keep the music students, no matter what their aims."

Chapter XV

"AN INCURABLE ROMANTIC"

All mankind loves a lover.
                              Ralph Waldo Emerson, *Love*

"A wedding, to Miss Baur, was always a champagne affair, no matter how simple," Miss Millie Muckerheide commented. "She liked to take full charge of the arrangements, managing everything herself, from selecting the trousseau to giving the bride away."

Miss Baur usually showed more than a passing interest in a courtship having its beginning on the Conservatory campus. She encouraged young lovers (and sometimes those not so young) to take the important step of marriage, often arranging for the ceremony to be held in her home or in the Conservatory parlors. There were many such weddings through the years, but the one which gave her the greatest pleasure was the marriage of her sister, Wanda Constance, to the eminent musician Chalmers Clifton.

For the beginning of this interesting romance, it is necessary to turn back the calendar to a day in September, 1903, when Chalmers Dancy Clifton enrolled as a student at the Cincinnati Conservatory of Music. His parents had intended that he follow the tradition of his family, pursuing a career in either medicine or the law. It is the Conservatory's good fortune that he responded to a stronger urge than the following of family tradition. By the time he entered the Conservatory, a slender, blond boy of thirteen-and-a-half, Chalmers Clifton was already a veteran of the concert stage, having given piano recitals in his native Mississippi since he was ten years of age. With her unerring foresight and her ability to assess a student's potential, Bertha Baur realized that here was genius. She was right, as usual, and in a few short years Mr. Clifton became a distinguished conductor and one of the representative American composers of his day.

97

In 1908 Chalmers Clifton graduated from the Conservatory with distinction. Then followed four years at Harvard University where he was accorded many honors: director of the Harvard Orchestra and chorister of the senior class. At the same time, he served on the editorial staff of numerous campus publications. While yet an undergraduate, he was selected to conduct the first MacDovell Festival at Petersboro, New Hampshire, in 1910. He also found time to orchestrate twenty of MacDowell's pieces for presentation at the festival.

Upon graduating *summa cum laude* from Harvard, Mr. Clifton went to Paris where he studied with Vincent d'Indy and Andre Gedlagé as the holder of a Sheldon traveling fellowship. In 1915 he returned to the United States, appearing as guest conductor in New York, Boston, and Cincinnati. He also composed and conducted the music for a pageant at Lexington, Massachusetts, commemorating 140 years of American independence.

During this time, the warm friendship formed earlier on the Conservatory campus continued to exist between the young Southerner and Wanda Baur. There was a lively exchange of letters and as many visits as Mr. Clifton's professional commitments would allow. Frequently, they were both invited for a visit with their mutual friend, Mrs. Mary Emery, at her estate, "Mariemont," in Newport. Mrs. Emery had, from the very beginning, shown a keen interest in Mr. Clifton's musical career, assisting him in every possible way.

Then came the First World War. Chalmers Clifton was appointed by Harvard to organize the New England branch of the American University Union in Paris. Subsequently, he enlisted in the intelligence bureau of the American Expeditionary Forces, was commissioned a first lieutenant, and cited by General John J. Pershing for "distinguished and meritorious service."

During the war, Lieutenant Clifton was signally honored by the French. He was asked to choose and conduct a program of American music with the *Societé des Concerts du Conservatoire*, the oldest orchestral body in the world, thus becoming the first American to direct this great French orchestra.

While serving his country in France, the correspondence

between Lieutenant Clifton and Wanda Baur assumed a more intimate role. Their friendship was ripening into a deeper relationship. "When the war is over," he confided to a friend, "I am going to ask Wanda to marry me."

Wanda Constance Baur was a gracious and friendly young woman, loved by everyone who knew her. Miss Marionbelle Blocksom remembers her as a "gentle girl with great dignity." Ray Staater, who knew her well, described her as a "wonderful girl, always kind and courteous, having a quiet reserve of strength that often went unnoticed." And yet, Miss Hattie Platter, Miss Bertha's executive assistant, confided to a co-worker that Miss Wanda "was not easy to work for;" that she "much preferred Miss Bertha."

Like most of the Baur women, Wanda was slender and petite, her delicate beauty having been compared to a "piece of fragile china." Her blonde hair, worn in a braided coronet around her head, was an inheritance from her Saxon ancestors, but her blue eyes, deep-pooled and exquisitely expressive, were a legacy from the Baurs.

Wanda Constance Baur and Chalmers Dancy Clifton were married on July 28, 1919, in the chapel of St. Savior of the Cathedral of St. John the Divine in New York City. The *Cincinnati Enquirer* observed: "Mrs. Clifton will be greatly missed here where she is a universal favorite."

A week before the wedding, Miss Bertha went to New York and took complete charge of the wedding arrangements, even selecting the trousseau. Miss Annie Howard remarked that "it was just as well, since Wanda was too far up in the clouds to be bothered with such a mundane chore as shopping."

Chalmers Clifton was perhaps the Conservatory's most distinguished alumnus. The *Musical Digest* called him "one of the rarely gifted musicians this country has produced." Although he was a prolific composer, his reputation rested upon his ability as a conductor. On one occasion, when he was guest conductor of the Boston Symphony Orchestra, the *Boston Transcript* called his reading of the Sibelius Second Symphony "music of flaming passion."

With his radiant good looks, his graceful posture, and prematurely white hair, Chalmers Clifton was an impressive figure on the podium. He directed with a total lack of histrionics, yet he was nonetheless masterful because of this quiet restraint. There was an effortless grace, an elegance of style, and a complete freedom from affectation in his conducting that was a pleasure to watch. Having total recall, Chalmers Clifton was one of the few leading conductors in the country who directed without a score. He remarked to Mrs. Hodges that a score was not necessary. "The notes march before my eyes like soldiers," he said.

In the years immediately following the war, Miss Baur was kept busy attending the weddings of her teaching staff. In the summer of 1923, Albert Berne, Cincinnati baritone and a member of the artist faculty, was married to Miss Lucille Kroger, daughter of B. H. Kroger, founder of the grocery chain that bears his name. This marriage was the highlight of the social season and took place at twilight on an evening in July on the lawn of the Kroger estate, "Yellow Oaks."

The next year, Miss Lucy de Young, Dan Beddoe's first assistant, became the bride of James Robertson Stewart, Cincinnati architect and builder. Miss de Young, a charming, brown-eyed redhead from Pennsylvania, was a member of the Summer Opera Company. With her magnificent contralto voice, she was always so busy rehearsing or performing that Mr. Stewart declared he had to "court her backstage between the acts where stagehands were moving scenery, carpenters were hammering, and the singers were vocalizing at the top of their lungs." Finally, he proposed to her one evening during an intermission as they strolled in the moonlight around the lake adjacent to the opera pavilion.

Of no less interest to Miss Baur was the announcement made simultaneously in Cincinnati and Berlin, of the approaching marriage of another member of her teaching staff: Louis John Johnen, prominent Cincinnati opera singer, teacher, and radio personality. While on leave of absence for further study in Berlin, he met a lovely German girl, Fräulein Lieselotte Proett, daughter of a distinguished Berlin artist. "It was love at first sight," Mr. Johnen said, "at least on my part. She was not easily persuaded to leave Germany, but I was persistent, and before I left for the United States she had given me her promise."

Miss Baur was especially pleased when she learned that Miriam Otto and Hubert Kockritz were planning a June wedding. Both of these young musicians were members of the Conservatory faculty and were highly regarded in Cincinnati music circles. Miss Otto, an exceptionally gifted pianist and accompanist, was a cousin of Bertha Baur on the maternal side. Mr. Kockritz, popular singer and opera coach, was one of her favorite young teachers. She insisted that the marriage take place in her home on the campus. She was absorbed for weeks in the preparations, and surely a more beautiful ceremony in its dignity and simplicity could not be imagined. A charming feature of this lovely wedding was the background music played by a trio of Miss Otto's associates at the Conservatory: Amy Lee, pianist; Jean Grubbs, violinist, and Marian Beers, cellist.

Other outstanding Conservatory teachers who took the important step of marriage during this time were: Daniel Ericourt, famous French pianist, whose lovely bride was Josephine McNamee, of Wabash, Indiana; Violet Summer, soprano, who married Dr. Charles F. Sherrick, Cincinnati dentist, and Madame Ruth Townsend, who chose as her groom the well-known Serbian baritone, Milan Petrovic, whom she had met while they were appearing in the same opera company in Paris.

Life at the Cincinnati Conservatory of Music was not, however, all champagne and bridal bouquets. Sorrow, disappointment, tragedy, and death cast their long shadows over the days. At times it seemed that Bertha Baur was called upon to bear more than the human heart could endure. Yet like her intrepid ancestors, she met each new crisis with courage and fortitude: a woman of steel whom nothing was able to defeat.

Why Bertha Baur never married was a favorite topic of conjecture among the students. Miss Annie Howard said that Miss Baur was "an incurable romantic, happiest when preparing for a wedding." Then she added, with a twinkle in her fine gray eyes, "provided it isn't her own."

At the beginning of each school year, rumors ran rife that a romantic attachment existed between Miss Baur and Frederic Shailer Evans. The legend was that they had been in love for years, but she had refused to marry him because she had promised Miss Clara that she would remain single and devote her life to the school. Each year the story was enhanced with additions and variatons, growing more and more poignant, until it rivaled the renunciation scene in *Traviata*. "It is just like a 'seven handkerchief' picture," declared a young drama student who had seen too many movies.

It was not difficult to understand why Miss Bertha might have been in love with Mr. Evans. With his craggy good looks and his courtly, Old World manner, he seemed to be surrounded by an aura of mystery. He was very much sought after by the ladies, but somehow had managed to avoid any sentimental entanglements. He was pleasant and courteous, but remote— except with Miss Baur. With her he was relaxed, smiling, and unhurried. From their vantage point in the office, the secretaries sometimes watched to see if they could detect a revealing expression when Mr. Evans came to her private office. "She might as well be talking to the gardener," Bertha Stahl flatly stated after a particularly disappointing vigil. Miss Marionbelle Blocksom had known them for many years and was sure they were only devoted friends. "Mr. Evans was loyal to her," Miss Blocksom said, "and Miss Bertha depended upon him for counsel and advice."

"The truth of the matter is," Mrs. Hodges said, "that a few years after Cousin Bertha came to the Conservatory, she had a serious love affair which ended in heartbreak." Miss Clara had engaged George Magrath, a brilliant young pianist from London, to be a member of her artist faculty. He had made an enviable reputation in Europe as a concert pianist, particularly as an interpreter of Liszt. He was enthusiastically received in Cincinnati and was in demand for social as well as musical events. But George Magrath remained impervious to the attentions of the debutantes and their ambitious mothers who tried to ensnare him. He had eyes only for Bertha Baur. From the very first meeting, there had been a mutual attraction. They discovered many similar tastes and viewpoints. Both were well versed in literature; both loved and admired the German musicians and poets, and both were fluent in languages. Said Mrs. Hodges: "He was the love of her life. She 'fell in love' for the first and only time."

Although no announcement had been made, Miss Bertha's

friends took the engagement for granted. She was seen everywhere in the company of Mr. Magrath: at concerts, musicales, the symphony, picnics, and excursions, yet the expected announcement was not forthcoming. No one in the Baur family seems to know why the marriage did not take place. The matter was never mentioned either by Miss Clara or Miss Bertha, but Ray Staater, who was in Miss Clara's confidence, stated that in spite of her high regard for the young pianist, she "simply would not allow it." Whatever the reason, Bertha Baur made what must have been the most difficult decision of her life.

Years later, one of Miss Baur's most generous gestures was made toward George Magrath's widow, who had lost her British citizenship during the war, reverting to the status of an Austrian citizen. Mrs. Magrath was attempting to visit her son, who was working for Vice President Calvin Coolidge in Washington. She was forced to spend intervals of six months in Canada, being permitted to return to Washington only at the end of those periods. As she was in failing health and had no friends in Canada, she appealed to Bertha Baur for help, since young Magrath did not wish to ask Mr. Coolidge for special favors. Miss Baur responded at once to her request, enlisting powerful friends in Washington to arrange for Mrs. Magrath to remain there near her son without being required to make periodic visits to Canada.

George Magrath was not the only man who courted Bertha Baur. Another member of the piano faculty (also an Englishman) came under her spell and, when she refused his proposal of marraige, he severed his ties with the Conservatory and returned to England. It was rumored that a noted Cincinnati physician was also one of her most devoted admirers.

"Cousin Bertha had many beaus and several proposals of marriage," Mrs. Hodges recalls, "but she did not seriously consider any of them. George Magrath was her one, her only love." To the end of her days she cherished a miniature of Mr. Magrath which she wore in a locket suspended from a chain around her neck. She would often hold the locket in her hand, fingering it gently. The lines of her face would soften, and a tender, faraway look would glow in her eyes as she held in her hand all that remained of a shattered dream.

Chapter XVI

TRADITIONS

Montrez-nous les écrins de vos riches mémoires,
Les bijoux marveilleux, faits d'astres et d'éthers.
Open for us the chest of your rich memories!
Show us those treasures, wrought of meteoric gold!
Baudelaire, *Flowers of Evil* (Dillon-Millay translation)

The traditions of a school are among its most precious possessions, creating a vast storehouse of memories to be cherished through the years.

Until it became a casualty of the automobile and the airplane, the Thanksgiving banquet was one of the most beautiful and inspiring of the Conservatory traditions. Since the schedule allowed for only one day, few students were able to go home and, indeed, few wanted to. The Misses Baur spared no effort to make this a truly memorable event. The dining room was lavishly decorated with autumn flowers and foliage, and the menu was unsurpassed. The place cards, designed especially for the occasion, were a work of art. After the banquet, those who wished to do so were permitted to attend the symphony or the theatre of their choice. Others assembled in the drawing rooms to visit with family and friends. All rules were suspended for the day. "Princess pitch" and "fairy footsteps" did not have to be observed too carefully.

"When the dining room was thrown open," said the 1909 winter issue of *Sharps and Flats*, "a sight of unsurpassed beauty was revealed. As if by magic the room had been transformed into an elaborately decorated banquet hall worthy of the feasts there on Thanksgiving Day."

"How I wish there had been color film in those days," Miss Flay Butler remarked recently. "It is a matter of great regret that future Conservatory students will never realize the beauty, brilliance, and charm of those bygone days."

104

One of the oldest and best-loved of the Conservatory traditions was the annual feast of carols which took place in December immediately preceding the Christmas recess. For more than three-quarters of a century the Conservatory has observed this impressive ceremony, each program seeming to be more beautiful than the last.

The first Christmas carol service was given in the historical McLean residence, the home of the Conservatory from 1892 until 1902. The original programs were given by a boys' choir from the Church of the Sacred Heart, under the direction of Dr. Harold Beckett Gibbs, organist and choirmaster of the church and head of the Conservatory's organ and choral departments. Miss Wanda Baur was the moving spirit in these festivities and, under her artistic hand, the drawing rooms were transformed into bowers of holiday greens, illuminated by the soft glow of candlelight. These lovely greens—holly, mistletoe, and juniper—were always sent by the Baur family in Michigan as a gift to the school. The young carolers, dressed in white vestments, came down the magnificent staircase singing the traditional carols of England and Germany. In later years, other features were added to the service, such as the little girls from Mrs. Pace's children's class and a group calling themselves the "Wassailers." One year, Mr. Karl Staps, choirmaster of the St. Paul's Cathedral, brought his junior choir to augment the original group.

A few years after the Conservatory moved to its new home on Highland Avenue, Dr. Thomas James Kelly took over the directing of the Christmas carols, using only the Conservatory students as choristers. At first the programs were presented in the foyer of Shillito Hall, with the singers grouped on the spacious, hand-carved staircase. Soon, however, these programs became so popular in the city that it was necessary to transfer them to the concert hall.

Dr. Kelly was a masterly musician, original, resourceful, and ingenious. While he had charge of the Feast of Carols, one could always look forward to something interesting and unusual in the programming. He included rare and uncommon carols from many lands, as well as the dear and familiar ones.

While doing research in London, Dr. Kelly happened upon the original manuscripts of a number of Old English carols:

"God Rest Ye Merry, Gentlemen," "Good King Wenceslas," and others. He was fascinated by the quaint phraseology and the interesting changes of word-meaning which have taken place through usage and translation. He received permission to make copies of some of these old manuscripts and later used them in narrating the carol programs.

No one seems to know when or how the Christmas carol program came to be known as a Feast of Carols. Mrs. Mary Pfau of the Conservatory voice faculty was sure it originated with Dr. Kelly. The title has a festive, joyous connotation and has persisted through the years, although many changes and innovations have taken place.

After Dr. Kelly retired from teaching, the carol service had other competent and creative directors, among whom were Dr. John A. Hoffmann, Willis Beckett, Elmer Thomas, and Dr. Lewis Whikehart.

Those of us who have had the privilege of being a part of this impressive pageant will always cherish the memory of a solemn and moving experience: the soft glow of candlelight, the spicy scent of evergreens, the expectant hush of the audience as the choristers, in immaculate white vestments, moved down the aisles singing the majestic "Adeste Fidelis," always used as the processional.

For many years attendance of the feast of carols was by invitation only, with two identical services given in the Conservatory concert hall. With each passing year, however, the requests for invitations became so great that even two performances were not sufficient to accommodate all those who wished to attend. It became necessary to seek larger quarters, and the Netherland Hotel's stately Hall of Mirrors was selected.

Since 1960, when the school became a part of the University of Cincinnati, this traditional service has been given on the university campus. In 1965 the university's modern dance group, under the direction of Lucette B. Comer, joined the choral groups in celebrating this beloved tradition. The College-Conservatory orchestra, directed by Thomas Mayer, and the brass choir, conducted by Ernest N. Glover, contributed the instrumental music for this occasion. It was an impressive performance, with near-perfection in every phase—musical, visual,

Cincinnati Conservatory of Music, Cincinnati, Ohio

and auditory—but a far cry from the original carol service as it was first presented in the McLean residence at Fourth and Lawrence Streets. The highlight of the 1965 performance was the Benjamin Britten cantata, *St. Nicholas*. As the dancers in their richly-colored costumes interpreted the scenes (sometimes with stark realism), one tried to visualize Miss Baur's reaction to this frank and vivid portrayal. Would she have approved of the startling innovations? The tight-fitting leotards? Who can tell? One thing is certain, however, she would not for one moment have dissembled. She would have expressed her opinion freely and without reservation.

The 1940 feast of carols was, appropriately, dedicated to the memory of Miss Baur, her death having occurred less than three months previously.

Commencement Week, with its nostalgic memories and highly-charged emotions, was a timely season in which to commemorate many of the Conservatory's cherished traditions. One of the most practical customs, as well as the most impressive, was observed by each outgoing senior class: the planting of a tree on the campus to stand as a living memorial to that particular class. This beautiful custom was inaugurated by Miss Clara in 1903 for the first class to be graduated in the new location. The graduates formed a procession at the entrance of Shillito Hall, then marched slowly across the campus to the site previously selected for the planting of the tree. The ceremonial spade, used annually, was kept from year to year by the president-elect of the senior class. It was decked with the colors of every preceding senior class, and the many-hued ribbons tied to its handle made a kaleidoscope of bright colors as they streamed in the wind and rippled to the motion of the spade.

The 1913 "Tree-Planting Day" was of special significance—the first tree-planting following the death of Miss Clara. The beautiful red-bud was dedicated to the memory of the Conservatory's beloved founder. Miss Bertha presided on this occasion, as she was to do for many years to come. Addressing the graduates, she reminded them that "the planting of the class tree was always considered by Miss Clara a great privilege, and formed each year a part of the vision which came to her many years ago when she founded the school.

"It may be a help to you to remember," Miss Bertha told the class, "when trials, tribulations, and discouragements come, as they do to all, that the many obstacles which had to be overcome by Miss Clara, as in the beautiful fable of the birds, grew to be the wings with which she soared."

The observance of Tree-Planting Day in 1927 was particularly impressive. It was a perfect June day, warm, sunny, and bright, with cottony white clouds drifting lazily across the blue sky. As the photographers focused their cameras on the scene, Miss Baur stepped forward, thrust the spade into the loosened earth, and cast the first soil around the roots of the trees. Then she stepped back, and in her beautiful melodious voice said:

> To me a tree is a living reminder of those hidden and eternal forces of life, compared to which mere human accomplishments are as the toys of a child. Silently and mysteriously it lives, a symbol of grace, beauty, and strength. May it help us to strive for the ideal which it attains—the union of beauty and strength.

It had been Miss Clara's original plan to form a "promenade" or avenue of trees extending across the campus, which subsequent classes would augment until the avenue should be complete. For some reason, however, the plan was not carried out.

As old as the school itself are the chamber music and ensemble groups. In the first catalog (1868-69), Miss Clara announced the formation of a chamber music group as an important part of the curriculum, a custom which she brought with her from Germany. True to the German fondness for group playing and singing, she hoped to create in her young American students the same love and enthusiasm that existed in her native country for this branch of music. From this small beginning came the Conservatory Symphony Orchestra, the symphonic band, the chorus, and the madrigal singers.

The madrigal singers, a mixed chorus of twenty voices, has always been one of the most professional groups on the campus. Its repertoire is performed *a cappella*, demanding a high proficiency in part singing. In 1939, under the direction of Dr. John A. Hoffmann, this talented group made an extensive tour, giving concerts in several large cities. In Washington, D.C., sponsored

109

by Ohio Senator Robert A. Taft and Mrs. Taft, they presented a program for the Ohio Society and were warmly applauded. The highlight of the tour was a program given before the Beethoven Association of New York, where no less an authority than Pitts Sanborn of the *New York World-Telegram* praised their "style and musicianship." The madrigal singers have also been featured on the Conservatory's Saturday morning broadcasts from the concert hall and on the Columbia Broadcasting Company's *Choral Quest* program.

For many years it was the custom early in December to erect a Christmas tree in the foyer of Shillito Hall. A magnificent cedar or spruce was selected personally by Miss Baur's brother Bertrand, and was shipped to her from his farm in Michigan. Students, faculty, alumni, and friends were invited to trim the tree with an offering for the benefit of the scholarship fund. It was a worthy tradition, attesting to the spirit of fellowship and solidarity which has always prevailed among Conservatory students wherever they may be found.

Through its long and illustrious history, the Cincinnati Conservatory of Music has had many cherished traditions, but the most precious ones that have come down through the years are its high ideals, moral integrity, and unsurpassed standards of scholarship.

Chapter XVII

"IN THE GRAND MANNER"

Doing easily what others find difficult is talent;
doing what is impossible for talent is genius.
Henri-Frédéric Amiel, *Journal*

The late Alfred Segal, reporter for the *Cincinnati Post and Times-Star*, whose column "Cincinnatus" was widely read and quoted, was one of Miss Baur's most fervent adherents. He spoke of her always with great affection, never ceasing to wonder at her vitality, strong intellect, and astounding qualities of leadership. "She carries herself like a queen," he remarked one evening as she came into the concert hall to attend a recital.

Bertha Baur was not a tall woman, but her erect posture and naturally regal bearing created the impression of greater height than she actually possessed. In the firm, buoyant step and the controlled motions of her body, one immediately sensed purpose and self-assurance. Mrs. Emery always referred to Miss Baur as "Miss Bertha," explaining that "one says 'Miss Bertha' as one would say 'Sir John' or 'Sir Charles'; as if addressing royalty."

Mrs. Samuel Besuner, of Cincinnati, whose daughters, Betty and Pearl, are distinguished musicians, recently remarked upon Miss Baur's dignity and charm. "The moment she came into a room," Mrs. Besuner said, "everyone seemed automatically to 'come to attention.' You were at once aware that you were in the presence of a compelling personality." Miss Pearl Besuner recalled that Miss Baur attended every recital. Standing in the vestibule of the concert hall before the appointed hour, she greeted visitors and friends, calling each one by name. Usually dressed in a crisp white gown, she was gracious and smiling, cool and immaculate even in the merciless heat of a Cincinnati summer.

Shortly after she took charge of the Conservatory, a reporter

111

of the New York *Musical Courier* was a visitor to the school. Miss Baur herself showed him about the buildings and grounds. "I cannot, of course, show you the girls' dormitories," she told him, "because that is where 'the angels dwell,' " In an editorial following his visit, the reporter described Miss Baur as "a woman of rare personal charm and distinction, who nevertheless betrays in her demeanor and speech the qualities that never are absent from the makeup of a successful executive."

To the casual observer, Bertha Baur appeared as a hard-working executive, engrossed in the management of her school to the exclusion of all else. While she worked long hours at her desk, and personally supervised every department of the Conservatory, somehow she found time to participate in a great number of organizations. One has only to glance at a partial list of her activities to understand the extent of her interests: The MacDowell Club, the *Alliance Française*, the National Federation of Music Clubs, the Cincinnati Woman's Club, the Matinee Musicale and the Mount Auburn Music Club. She also served on the executive boards of the Cincinnati Symphony Orchestra, the Cincinnati Art Museum, and the Cincinnati Public Recreation Commission.

Miss Baur's long-time friend, Will Reeves, was director of the recreation commission at the same time that she was on the executive board. During his tenure of office he inaugurated a series of "street shows" to bring entertainment to the inner-city areas. On summer evenings, certain streets were closed to traffic, and entertainers performed from improvised platforms. He stated that it was "due to Miss Baur's cooperation in providing talent from the Conservatory that these programs were possible."

Miss Baur's energy and capacity for work seems incredible when it is remembered that aside from the relentless demands of her official duties, she constantly had to attend recitals, fulfill speaking engagements, and receive and entertain countless visitors. In addition, she was active in many charitable organizations, including those of Christ Church, where she was a regular communicant. How she was able to keep this grueling pace is a mystery. A lesser person would have quailed before such a strenuous schedule.

"She was a remarkable woman of great stamina, demanding from her students and from her associates alike the same discipline she exacted of herself," Mrs. Dorothy (Hull) Beatty recalls. "She was a handsome woman of great charm and dignity who never seemed to evince any weariness." Mrs. Beatty, who is a Conservatory graduate, was a pupil of Theodor Bohlmann. She is a well-known concert pianist and makes her home in California.

By the early twenties, Miss Baur's once red-gold hair was snow-white, enhancing the beauty of her youthful complexion and adding to her look of distinction. Miss Millie Muckerheide remarked that "Miss Bertha's flawless complexion never needed make-up" and her "lovely hair was so easy to manage." Then she added with an amused smile, "But, oh, those high-button shoes. How I dreaded to fasten all those buttons." Miss Baur was not a slave to the whims of fashion. In fact, she paid little attention to the changing styles. "Like the late Queen Mary of England," said Alice Baur Hodges, "Cousin Bertha created her own individual style, succeeding in being appropriately dressed on all occasions."

Sitting on the sun porch of her home on Highland Avenue near the site of the "Old Conservatory," Miss Muckerheide recalled the days when she served on Miss Baur's domestic staff. She said that before South Hall was purchased by the school, Miss Baur gave large, fashionable teas in the drawing room of the Burnet House in downtown Cincinnati. On these occasions Miss Baur presided at the tea table, pouring from a handsome copper samovar, an heirloom which her grandmother Herzer brought from Saxony.

"It was my duty to go with Miss Baur to these parties," Miss Muckerheide said, "because I was the only one of her staff who was able to manage that balky samovar!" She also remembered that the more intimate teas and dinners were given in Shillito Hall. "My! but there were gay parties in those days!" she exclaimed, her bright black eyes twinkling with amusement.

One of Miss Baur's outstanding talents—showmanship—was seldom recognized, so skillfully and subtly was it employed. She had the inimitable gift of taking the commonplace and turning it into a rare and exciting experience. Even in the simple announcement of a social event or a concert, her voice was so vibrant, so lively, and her enthusiasm so contagious, that one fairly tingled with anticipation.

In the opinion of Peter Froehlich of the theory department, the most artistic and original program ever presented by the Cincinnati Woman's Club was devised by Miss Baur and executed under her expert direction. "Nothing like it had ever been seen in Cincinnati," he stated.

The program was designed to portray a painting by V. de Parades, showing Karl Philipp Emanuel Bach seated at the piano, surrounded by the gentlemen of the court in fascinating eighteenth-century dress. The animating of this famous painting was accomplished by a series of tableaux, the scenes "coming to life" as participants performed the music of the period. With the assistance of several Conservatory teachers and the cooperation of the club members, the music, the costumes, and the customs of the court of Frederick the Great of Prussia were revived. K.P.E. Bach, court musician to the king, was impersonated by Theodor Bohlmann; King Frederick, himself a composer and accomplished flutist, was portrayed by Ellis McDiarmid, flutist of the Cincinnati Symphony, while the role of royal orchestra conductor was assumed by Pier Adolfo Tirindelli. Included in the numbers were a Bach concerto, Handel's *Overture to Almira*, and a sonata for violin and piano, played by Mr. Bohlmann and Mr. Tirindelli.

"The final number of the program," reported the May, 1914 issue of *Sharps and Flats*, was the *Minuette in E-flat major* by Haydn. As the measured melody pictured the snuff-box, paint and patches, there drifted out upon the stage an octet of dames and courtiers who moved to the slow steps and deep curtsies of this older day with amazing fidelity. . . . With their last flutter of fan and point of slipper, the past drew back to its own again, and the eighteenth century gave place to the twentieth as the hostesses of the evening received the members of the club and their guests in honor of the artists who had made possible so unique and fascinating an hour."

Another memorable event arranged by Miss Baur was a music festival given for the purpose of raising funds for the Edward MacDowell Memorial Association. Miss Clara had been an admirer of Edward MacDowell's compositions and a close friend of his wife, and had been the prime mover in organizing the MacDowell Society in Cincinnati. In fact, the plans for the Society were made in the drawing room of Shillito Hall, with Miss Clara Baur presiding, less than a month before her death.

Miss Bertha gave as much time to the MacDowell Society as her schedule allowed, remembering how much it had meant to her aunt and to Mrs. MacDowell. When called upon to help make the festival a success, she responded, as usual, with an exciting and original contribution to the program. She assembled sixteen of the finest pianists of the country in a mass performance of sixteen grand pianos on the stage of Music Hall. The ensemble was directed by Fritz Reiner, then conductor of the Cincinnati Symphony Orchestra. It was indeed a novelty, and created a sensation in music circles. Never before had Cincinnatians seen such a large number of pianos assembled on stage at one time and played en masse. Of the sixteen pianists, all but three were Conservatory faculty members, and those three—Dwight Anderson, Florence Barbour and Faye Ferguson—were Conservatory graduates. The other pianists were: Alma Betcher, Maria Carreras, Karin Dayas, Daniel Ericourt, Marguerite Melville Liszniewska, Karol Liszniewski, Misczyslaw Munz, Leo Paalz, Martin Read, Jr., Louis Saverne, Rudolph Thomas, Jemmie Vardeman and Thomie Prewett Williams. Smaller ensembles made up most of the program—duos, trios, and quartettes—the sixteen players combining only for the opening and closing numbers. The performance of Schubert's "Marche Militaire" by the sixteen pianists was the feature of the program, with the women concertists playing the upper part and the men the lower. "Accuracy and frequent brilliance of playing signalized the music, as was only to be anticipated from the distinguished position which the assisting artists occupy in the realm of music," said Nina Pugh Smith of the *Cincinnati Times-Star*. Miss Baur was so anxious that the entire proceeds of the concert might be used for the benefit of the MacDowell Society that she donated the use of the Music Hall. The participating musicians, following her lead, contributed their services.

Bertha Baur was never known to do anything by halves. As

the editor-in-chief of the *New York Musical Courier* so aptly put it: "Nothing ever undertaken by the Cincinnati Conservatory of Music and its head, Miss Bertha Baur, is done in anything but the grand manner."

Chapter XVIII
"A MASTER OF ARTS — AND ARTISTS"

. . . honor to whom honor is due.
Romans 13:7 (RSV)

The University of Cincinnati was among the first institutions of higher learning to recognize Bertha Baur's significant contributions to music education in this country. Her progressive leadership, particularly in the field of public school music, had merited the commendation of eminent educators and professionals both at home and abroad. Wishing to make public acknowledgement of Miss Baur's achievements, the university requested the privilege of conferring upon her the honorary degree of Master of Arts. It was an impressive ceremony and took place at the university's commencement exercises on June 13, 1925, a memorable event and one of Miss Baur's most treasured moments.

Commencement morning was clear, bright, and sparkling. Sunlight shone warmly on the soft green grass and touched the topmost boughs of the stately old trees. A warm summer breeze with sudden gusts sent robes billowing and set the tassels on mortarboards dancing. At the appointed hour the traditional academic procession wound its way from historic McMicken Hall to the gymnasium, where the exercises were to be held. The long line of graduates, the largest graduating class in the history of the university, resplendent in cap and gown, were solemn in their newly-acquired dignity. Cameras clicked and flashbulbs popped as parents, newsmen, and friends captured on film a lasting record of this important day. Inside the gymnasium the excited hum of voices made a pleasantly confused sound, ceasing abruptly as the procession entered the hall.

One of the anticipated features of the program was the conferring of honorary degrees upon a number of educators whose accomplishments had been noteworthy. Among those to be so

117

honored was Miss Bertha Baur.[1] Sponsoring her as a candidate for the degree was Dr. Frank Chandler, dean of the College of Liberal Arts. Presenting her to the University's president, Dr. Frederick C. Hicks, Dr. Chandler had this to say:

> Mr. President, a city is not made by brick and stone merely; it is made by its finest men and women. They signify far more than all its material possessions; for they constitute its very soul. In that faith the university delights to honor those who have wrought their lives into the spiritual fabric of this community; those who have contributed to its cultural supremacy.
>
> One such citizen I would present to you today—a woman of remarkable ability and charm, distinguished for private and for civic virtues, a fosterer and patron of the arts, known everywhere for her devotion and service to the cause of music. Through her unflagging zeal and unaided by endowment, the Cincinnati Conservatory of Music has become one of the great institutions of its kind in this country, influential at home and abroad wherever music is loved.
>
> Mr. President, as you know, it is hard enough to administer even a university, but successfully to develop and administer a Conservatory of Music, with its coruscating galaxy of temperamental artists, deserves not a degree, but a *crown*.
>
> By reason of her knowledge, tact, and gracious personality, Miss Bertha Baur has achieved the impossible—from potential discord she has wrought perfect harmony. It is with peculiar pleasure, therefore, that, on behalf of the senate of the University, I recommend her to you for the honorary degree Master of Arts—and—may I add—artists!

Bertha Baur was now at the peak of her career, strong in body and mind, sure of herself and her direction. Her name had become synonymous with the great school she had helped to build. She was constantly in demand to speak before educational, civic, and religious organizations, and now that she had the assistance of Mr. Tuthill in the management of the school, she was able more often to accept these engagements.

When the city of Philadelphia celebrated its Sesquicentennial in 1926, Miss Baur was unanimously awarded the medal for the Ohio woman who had made the greatest contribution to the realm of music. "We rode with Governor Donahey in the Ohio parade," Miss Baur related, "with the wonderful Cleveland Grays Band and the soldiers leading." Both Miss Baur and Governor Donahey spoke on Ohio Day when the state flags were presented to the Court of Honor. Miss Baur was extremely

Miss Bertha Baur shortly after she received the degree, Master of Arts, from the University of Cincinnati, in June 1925

gratified that Bruce Carey, at that time a member of the Conservatory faculty, was chosen to direct the Sesquicentennial's large chorus of selected voices, thus bringing further honors to the school.

On the second day of the exposition, Miss Baur was the guest of honor at a special luncheon given by the women members of the Exposition Commission. At this event she received signal recognition by the master of ceremonies as "one of Ohio's most able and distinguished citizens." And the *Musical Courier* observed: "Some few personalities force an exposition to blazon forth their deeds to the world. Such a personality is Miss Bertha Baur."

On the last day of their attendance at the exposition, the Ohio women were taken on a tour of the city. They visited Independence Hall and other historical sites, and were entertained at a luncheon at Valley Forge. Miss Baur said of this occasion: "We dined bountifully on the spot where Washington and his revolutionary army once nearly starved."

A few months following Miss Baur's memorable visit to Philadelphia, she was accorded still another honor at the annual meeting of the conference of Southern Music School Supervisors in Louisville, Kentucky. She was guest of honor at the banquet and made the principal address to the members. Dr. Frederick A. Cowles, then president of the Louisville Conservatory of Music, introduced her to the membership, commending her upon the "splendid training and the high caliber of graduates sent out from the Conservatory into the teaching profession."

In April 1927, when the Ohio Music Teachers' Association met in Cincinnati, Miss Baur was appointed chairman of the banquet for the members of the association. The *Musical Leader* remarked upon her "radiant, inspiring beauty and her melodious speaking voice as she graciously introduced the speakers of the evening." In June of that year, she was guest of honor at the graduation exercises of Lindenwood College, St. Charles, Missouri, in which a large number of teachers in the music department were Conservatory graduates.

The honor that touched Miss Baur more deeply perhaps than all the others was a plaque presented to her by the Alumni

Association in recognition of her accomplishments and her years of faithful service to the school. Sherwood Kains, president of the association at that time, made the presentation in a simple but moving ceremony in Shillito Hall. Bearing the legend, "By their fruits ye shall know them," the plaque now hangs on the wall near the entrance to the Baur Room in the new College-Conservatory of Music on the campus of the University of Cincinnati.

Bertha Baur did not seek these honors and, indeed, she did not want them, but graciously accepted unless she suspected exploitation of the Conservatory's prestige. In that event, the refusal came promptly and with none too good grace.

If one imperfection marred the disposition of this unusual woman, it was her hair-trigger temper, which, seemingly, she made little effort to control. When she was angry or frustrated, she inflicted her mood on those around her, usually the first person she met. As one of her office staff remarked, she simply had to "get it out of her system."

Miss Millie Muckerheide recalls that Miss Baur was "extremely irritable" when things went wrong. "As soon as she came home at night, I could tell if her day had been unusually trying," Miss Muckerheide said. "She would be in a bad humor and nothing pleased her." Fortunately, this little German girl had the happy faculty of understanding Miss Baur's temperament and knew how to deal with her moods. "I simply kept quiet," she said, "and soon her bad mood would blow over."

It was no secret that Bertha Baur often lost her temper and lashed out at anyone who dared cross her. Yet she could be completely self-contained if the occasion demanded. When, to gain her ends, it was necessary to use her naturally persuasive powers, she was a master of diplomacy. She seemed to know intuitively when to scold, cajole, persuade, or command. She handled intractable persons with such finesse that they often capitulated without realizing they had been "maneuvered."

"In my opinion, Miss Baur's temper tantrums were greatly exaggerated," George Duly said recently. "In all the years I worked for her she never gave me an unkind word." Occasionally, George acted as her chauffeur and also waited on the table in her private dining room. "If she happened to be cross or moody," he said, "no one took offense. All of us knew that in trouble or illness we could always count on Miss Bertha."

James Doty, George's father, was a familiar figure at the Conservatory for many years. As head maintenance man, he was the embodiment of efficiency, dignity, and kindness. Miss Baur often said she "couldn't run the school without James."

In her capacity as housekeeper and dietitian, Mrs. Della Gabriel probably felt the sting of Miss Baur's criticisms more often than anyone else on the staff, since students the world over reserve the privilege to complain about the food. Conservatory students were no exception, and this annoyed Miss Baur out of all proportion to its significance. Mrs. Gabriel's sister, Mrs. Cecil Hall, of Cincinnati, said, "My sister was kind, gentle and understanding, and held no resentment against Miss Baur for these outbursts. She continued to serve the school faithfully until her retirement, in spite of the fact that her family constantly urged her to resign."

Mrs. Gabriel came to the Conservatory in 1921 from the Burnet House where she had filled the position of housekeeper. Located on the northwest corner of Third and Vine Streets, the Burnet House was at that time considered Cincinnati's finest hotel and was famous throughout the Midwest for its elegant appointments and excellent cuisine.

At the time Mrs. Gabriel came to the school, George Bowman, head waiter at the Burnet House, was employed by Miss Baur to assume the same position at the Conservatory. In his opinion, Miss Baur could do no wrong. "She was the kindest, the most considerate person I have ever met," he said. "She tried to give the best possible musical education to all the students and, to do this, she traveled both at home and abroad to secure the best teachers." He also recalled that on occasions when she was extremely busy, she would "forget to come to her meals." Then kindly, thoughtful George would take a tray to her office, gently reminding her that she had forgotten to come to the dining room. Like most of her domestic staff, Mr. Bowman remained in Miss Baur's service until her death. After he left the Conservatory, he entered the ministry and is now a bishop in the Cincinnati Christ Temple Church.

Miss Baur's eyes, clear and luminous, were the most revealing feature of her face. They would cloud with compassion as she shared the sorrows and misfortunes of others; they would glow with pride as she listened to the accomplishments of her pupils; or they would suddenly become rapier-keen and cold as ice when she was angry.

Only one of Miss Baur's employees openly defied her and got away with it, at least within the memory of the Conservatory staff. Never in the history of the school had there been such a confrontation. Miss Baur had entrusted a variety of duties to a spirited young lady from the East: chaperoning, typing, and operating the switchboard, among other things. One day, Miss Baur took her to task for some slight infraction of the rules, unjustly, the young lady thought. Instead of remaining silent under the rebuke, as most people did, she looked Miss Baur in the eye and said, "You go to hell." The office staff, fascinated witnesses to this clash of wills, waited apprehensively for the explosion which was sure to come. However, seeing that she had come off second best, Miss Baur put her head in her hands and shook with laughter.

Chapter XIX

GENIUS ON THE TEACHING STAFF

Genius hath electric power
Which earth can never tame. . . .
Lydia Maria Child, *Marius Amid the Ruins of Carthage*

The Cincinnati Conservatory of Music, with its faculty of varied nationalities and divergent backgrounds, always had its quota of fascinating, and sometimes eccentric, personalities—eminently qualified, often temperamental, occasionally difficult, but never dull. Bertha Baur had the inimitable gift of discovering and acquiring for her teaching staff some of the most renowned, as well as the most colorful, artists in the music world. This was the "leaven in the loaf" that made the Conservatory one of the finest music schools of its time.

Eugène Ysaÿe

Undoubtedly, the most notable of these artists was Ysaÿe, world-famous violinist, whose dazzling technique was sheer magic. While serving as conductor of the Cincinnati Symphony Orchestra, he taught a master class at the Conservatory which Miss Baur described as "not mere lessons, but veritable experiences in musical culture." To have secured the "Colossus of the Violin" as a member of her teaching staff was a stroke of genius on the part of Bertha Baur. Ysaÿe not only was a famous violinist, he was also an eminent conductor and a teacher of force and ability. His pupils adored him.

Arthur Bowen, a member of the Cincinnati Symphony during Ysaÿe's tenure, stated that "it was a privilege to have been in the orchestra when this celebrated musician was its conductor." Herbert Silbersack, who played with the orchestra for almost fifty years, spoke with affection of his former conductor. "We all loved him," Mr. Silbersack said. "Being primarily an artist, Ysaÿe was not a strict disciplinarian."

124

While it was true that Eugène Ysaÿe did not enforce strict discipline in his orchestra, he demanded perfection from his studio accompanists. Upon his arrival at the Conservatory, he auditioned and rejected, with a great display of temperament, at least three potential accompanists for his master class. Miss Baur was in despair. One day, however, Miss Fern Sherman, a young pianist of unusual ability, was passing through Cincinnati and, having a few hours between trains, took advantage of the time to visit her sorority sisters at the Conservatory. Miss Baur happened to hear her play and decided that she must audition for Ysaÿe. Miss Sherman explained that she had accepted a scholarship in another school and must leave at once. "You will have a scholarship here," Miss Baur said. In vain did Miss Sherman protest that she would miss her train. Miss Baur was not to be diverted and, almost before she knew what had happened, Miss Sherman found herself playing for the famous violinist.

While she auditioned, her friends halfheartedly played croquet on the lawn near Ysaÿe's studio. The croquet game was, however, only a listening post. The girls were waiting to offer comfort and consolation to Miss Sherman when Ysaÿe dismissed her from his presence as he had all the others. No such thing happened. Ysaÿe, beaming his approval, escorted Miss Sherman to the croquet court to rejoin her friends, while Miss Baur, smiling and happy, announced that she had, at last, found an accompanist to meet the requirements of the great Belgian master.

Eugène Ysaÿe was born in Liège, Belgium, on July 16, 1858. He made his first concert appearance when he was only seven, but his genius was not recognized until his late twenties. His recognition came as the result of his friendship with Hugo Heermann, long before Mr. Heermann came to Cincinnati as concertmaster of the Cincinnati Symphony. Because his own reputation as a musician was firmly established in Germany, Mr. Heermann was able to assist Ysaÿe in securing the position of violin soloist with the Frankfort-Am-Main orchestra, of which Mr. Heermann was concertmaster. This gave the young violinist's career its much-needed impetus.

When Ysaÿe came to Cincinnati in 1918 to take charge of the Cincinnati Symphony, Cincinnatians recalled that this was not his first visit to the Queen City. In 1894 he had made a tour of the leading music centers of this country, and Cincinnati was included in his itinerary. In November of that year, he appeared as soloist with the Orpheus Club. Apparently, concertgoers were not greatly impressed at this time by the performance of the young violinist whose artistry, years later, "took the country by storm." The Cincinnati press made only a routine mention of the concert.

It would be impossible to describe the mysterious loveliness of Ysaÿe's tone. He would sometimes take his own instrument and demonstrate the correct execution of a passage, and students who were passing his studio would pause to listen, drawn irresistibly by the sublime beauty of his tone. Miss Baur came nearest, perhaps, to the perfect description of his artistry: "The notes were so rich, so round, so mellow, and golden that I could almost reach out and hold them in my hand," she said.

Ysaÿe's resignation in 1923 as conductor of the Cincinnati Symphony Orchestra was received with genuine regret by music lovers, not only in Cincinnati, but throughout the Midwest. Miss Baur was distressed over this turn of events and urged Ysaÿe to reconsider, but he was adamant. It was rumored that he had demanded that certain concessions be made to his son, Gabriel, who was also a violinist and a member of the orchestra. When these demands were refused, Ysaÿe, in a mood of pique, resigned. There were also rumors that this was not the whole story; that he felt slighted because he had not been invited to conduct the 1923 May Festival, but this was only conjecture.

This immortal genius, before whom kings and queens had bowed in homage, died in Brussels on May 12, 1931, within a few months of his seventy-third birthday. Ysaÿe's body lay in state while thousands, including representatives of foreign countries, came to pay him honor. Near the casket, at his head, was placed his priceless Guarnerius violin, the instrument with which he had enthralled the world. After an impressive Gregorian Mass was said, Queen Elizabeth of Belgium led the procession to the Ixelles Cemetery, where his body was interred.

Dan Beddoe

Dan Beddoe, known as "the greatest oratorio singer of all

126

time," came to the Conservatory in 1919 from New York City where he had maintained his professional headquarters for almost ten years. He was past fifty at the time, well beyond the age when most singers have passed their peak and have retired from public performance, yet his voice had retained the freshness and vigor of a man half his age. "The years have dealt kindly with Mr. Beddoe's voice as time might wear a silver coin bright but thin," said *The New York Times*, following his appearance in the *Messiah* with the Oratorio Society of New York in December, 1933.

One of Mr. Beddoe's most notable performances was given during the 1931 Cincinnati May Festival. He was in his sixties and had not been well the previous winter. It was doubtful that he would be able to appear at all, and had not allowed his name to be placed on the program. At the last moment, however, he felt sufficiently recovered to sing in the closing concert. At the conclusion of the stirring aria, "Onaway! Awake! Beloved!" of Coleridge Taylor, he was accorded a thunderous ovation unparalleled in the memory of Cincinnati concertgoers. One critic said of the occasion: "the house rose to a man to applaud . . . the white-haired, stocky, pink-cheeked little Welshman who had brought to the festival its until then lacking touch of vocal glory which Mr. Beddoe always imparted to any performance in which he sang."

Dan Beddoe was born in the quaint little village of Aberdare, Glamorganshire, South Wales. He used to say, with a twinkle in his merry blue eyes, that he was fortunate not to have been born in a nearby village which boasted the longest name ever to be listed in a geography. The name of the village? Llanfairpwllgwyngyllgogerychwyrndrobwll-llandysiliogogogoch! His long and amazing career began when he won first prize at the Eisteddfods Festival in Wales when he was only eighteen years of age. In that contest (1885), the test piece was a difficult aria, "Through the Forests," by Weber. From the moment his clarion tones ran out, the judges knew that here was a voice unsurpassed in the annals of the Eisteddfods. The coveted first prize unquestionably belonged to the young tenor from Aberdare in spite of the large number of professional singers competing against him. To win the first place in the National Eisteddfods is to capture the highest national honor to which an artist may aspire.

Following a concert tour in England, Mr. Beddoe appeared with the Royal Welsh Prize Singers in a number of American cities. At the conclusion of this engagement, he returned to Wales and, in his own words, "married the only sweetheart I ever had." Shortly afterward, he brought his bride to the United States to make their home. The Beddoes were the parents of two children, Gladys Dante (Mrs. James Vermilya), and a son, Don, now a well-known actor making his home in Hollywood.

Dan Beddoe died suddenly in New York City, December 26, 1937. Although he had become internationally famous, he never lost the common touch nor the childlike simplicity that made him one of the most beloved artists of his time.

Chevalier Pier Adolfo Tirindelli

Pier Adolfo Tirindelli was born in Conegliano, Italy, May 5, 1858. Very early in life his musical talent became apparent and he was entered in the Conservatory of Music at Milan. Later, he studied in Vienna where he met the great pianist Liszt, who gave the young violinist encouragement. After a few years' study in Vienna, Tirindelli returned to Venice to direct the Venetian Symphony and also to take charge of the violin department of the Music Lycée. During this period he led a busy life musically, composing and conducting, teaching, and giving command performances for Queen Margherita and the Duke and Duchess of Genoa when Their Highnesses were in residence in Venice.

Although Tirindelli had been acclaimed in his own country and had been knighted with the Order of Crown of Italy of King Humberto, he was restless and discontented. Feeling that great opportunities were to be found in the United States, he gave up his work in Venice and sailed for Boston. He was influenced, no doubt, in his choice of location by the attractive and vivacious Isabella Stewart Gardner (Mrs. John Lowell Gardner), of Boston, whom he met in Venice in 1892 and for whom he had a great admiration. At the time he met the Gardners, they were spending the winter in Venice. Tirindelli was often a guest in their luxurious villa where he was the featured performer in many of Mrs. Gardner's fashionable musicales.

Upon Tirindelli's arrival in Boston in 1896, he was introduced by the Gardners into their circle of friends. He was one of a select group of musicians who were often asked to perform at Mrs. Gardner's "evenings of music," which she had made popular in Boston. Almost at once he secured a position in the Boston Symphony Orchestra, conducted at that time by Wilhelm Gericke. It was not many months until he was appointed concertmaster of the orchestra.[1] Yet in spite of his favorable reception in Boston, once again he became restless and discontented. In the summer of 1898 he severed his connection with the Boston Symphony. It was Miss Baur's good fortune that he accepted the position as head of the violin department of the Cincinnati Conservatory of Music.

Tirindelli's reputation as a musician had preceded him and he was warmly welcomed by music-conscious Cincinnati. Mr. Herbert Silbersack recently reminisced about the days when he studied with this distinguished violinist. "He was a wonderful teacher," Mr. Silbersack said. "I was only fourteen or fifteen years old when I started studying with him and his outwardly stern demeanor scared me at first. His English wasn't very good and we didn't always understand each other, but after awhile we got together." Mr. Silbersack recalled that he played solo violin when the Conservatory orchestra performed Mr. Tirindelli's composition, *Concerto for Violin and Orchestra*, with the composer on the podium.

Caruso, who recognized Tirindelli's genius, often included his songs on both his American and European concert programs. Tirindelli's one-act opera, *Blanc et Noir*, was given its première in Cincinnati and was considered a great triumph for the composer.

The Tirindellis were the parents of two lovely daughters, Margherita and Wanda, the latter being named in honor of Wanda Constance (Baur) Clifton. Both daughters were accomplished singers, Margherita possessed a beautiful lyric soprano, trained at the Conservatory under the guidance of the eminent opera singer Minnie Tracey. In 1919, Wanda made her debut on Broadway in the musical extravaganza, *Chu Chin Chow*. After one season in New York, however, she returned to Italy where

129

she was married to the Marquis di Simeri (Count Curci), former husband of the world-famous singer Galli-Curci.

The following year, Chevalier and Madame Tirindelli also returned to Italy to make their home. Pier Adolfo Tirindelli died in Rome on February 6, 1937, two months before his seventy-ninth birthday.

John A. Hoffmann

Dr. John A. Hoffmann was considered one of the finest vocal teachers in the country. Opera, radio, television and the concert stage, as well as colleges and universities, have been enriched by the men and women who were trained by this inspiring teacher. He won the respect of the public and the love and trust of his students by his scrupulous honesty and the sterling quality of his work.

Dr. Hoffmann was a musician of astonishing versatility. He had a wide knowledge of piano, organ, and violin, as well as vocal culture and choral conducting. His earliest ambition was to be a concert pianist, but Miss Clara Baur discovered that he had a voice of rare lyric quality and urged him to change the emphasis of his course of study to the art of singing. Under her personal tutelage, he pursued the study of voice, graduating from the Conservatory with high honors. He then went to Europe for postgraduate work. Upon his return to Cincinnati in 1910, Miss Clara invited him to become a member of the Conservatory voice faculty.

While concertizing in London, Mr. Hoffmann was accorded an unusual honor. His niece, Mrs. John W. Hauser, tells the story: "My uncle gave a command performance at Buckingham Palace before the King and Queen of England and other crowned heads of the Empire. Their Majesties were so impressed by his remarkable musicianship that they presented him, as a token of appreciation, with a stone from the robe of King Richard III. Later, he had the jewel mounted in a ring for Mrs. Hoffmann, who wore it until her death." The ring is now in the possession of Mrs. Hauser.

In September, 1913, Mr. Hoffmann was married to Miss Minna Wagner, of Cincinnati, a vivacious young woman with sparkling brown eyes and a warm, outgoing personality. Prominent in the music affairs of the city and the state, she shared her husband's enthusiasm for all things musical. As president of the Cincinnati Federation and of the Ohio Federation of Music Clubs, she assisted many young musicians to attain recognition.

Dr. Hoffmann died suddenly in the summer of 1946, having served the school faithfully and well for thirty-six years, first as a teacher, then as dean, and finally as director. There was widespread grief for the loss of this beloved teacher who had devoted his life to the training of young musicians. Said the *Cincinnati Times Star*: "Many thousands of Cincinnatians and musicians in all parts of the country thought of Dr. Hoffmann as 'Dean of Music.' "

Dr. Hoffmann's portrait, painted by Norbert Heermann, the gift of alumni and friends, hangs near the Baur Room in the College-Conservatory of Music. Mrs. Hoffmann's portrait, painted by Mrs. Stella Fabian Linville, a local artist, hangs beside that of her distinguished husband.

Edgar Stillman-Kelley

Edgar Stillman-Kelley, composer, musicologist and author, took charge of the Conservatory's theoretical department in 1911. "Dr. Kelley is a man to whom the musical world of all countries may point with pride," wrote the *New York Musical Leader* of July 13, 1911. "Many institutions of this country and of Europe will, with good reason, envy Cincinnati its acquisition."

Dr. Kelley was one of the most versatile composers of his day, having created a large variety of pieces from suites to symphonies. He explained his compositions to his pupils by saying that he translated into music each new experience in life. His *New England Symphony*, for instance, depicted the beauties of the region of his birth; Bunyan's *Pilgrim's Progress* so impressed him that he made it the basis of a complex work for orchestra, chorus, and soli. It was given its première at the 1918 May Festival under the baton of Eugène Ysaÿe. "*Alice in Wonderland* attracted me," he said, "as it does all lovers of the fanciful, so I put her into a little orchestra suite." Shakespeare's plays also appealed to Dr. Kelley as themes for his compositions. "I experienced pleasure in imagining fantastic settings for the various scenes, particularly of *Macbeth* and *A Midsummer-Night's Dream*," he said.

His intensive research in Chinatown (San Francisco), interviewing its inhabitants and listening to the ancient Chinese melodies resulted in his Chinese suite, *Aladdin*. His *Musical Instruments*,[2] a comprehensive history of the origin and development of musical instruments, is still in use as a reference work.

Dr. Kelley was a kind and gentle man, seemingly detached from the everyday world. He was known to be extremely absentminded, especially when he was in the throes of creating a new work. He became so absorbed that time ceased to exist and he was, literally, oblivious to the elements. Amusing anecdotes about this endearing trait were constantly repeated. One beautiful spring morning, so the story goes, Dr. Kelley started across the campus wearing a raincoat and a battered old rain hat, holding an open umbrella. Mrs. Kelley, ever the watchful, solicitous wife, called to him and asked why he was dressed in his rainwear. Dr. Kelley smiled uncertainly and held out his hand to gauge the weather. "Oh, yes, dear," he answered, "I remember now. It was *yesterday* that it rained."

The Kelleys had no children and all of Mrs. Kelley's maternal instincts were lavished on her "darling Edgar." She was constantly by his side, making sure he met his classes and was on time for his appointments. Mrs. Kelley was, herself, a fine musician and she and Dr. Kelley jointly taught several calsses in theory and harmony. They often argued in these classes about points upon which they did not agree. In one instance, they were so absorbed in a discussion of the art of notation that neither of them heard the dismissal bell. The class heard it, needless to say, and one by one stepped quietly out of the room until no one remained except, of course, Dr. and Mrs. Kelley, still arguing.

This beloved man, whose devotion to music had been an inspiration to many young artists, died in New York City on November 12, 1944, in his eighty-seventh year.

Chapter XX

THE ROARING TWENTIES

The hangover became a part of the day as
well allowed-for as the Spanish siesta.
F. Scott Fitzgerald, *My Lost City*

The 1920s were a period of unprecedented growth for the Cincinnati Conservatory of Music, a brilliant epoch in its history. With a faculty of world-renowned artists, a complex of five magnificent buildings, and the largest student body on record, the school reached the zenith of its cultural influence. This was the decade known as the Roaring Twenties or the Jazz Age—a restless, flamboyant era in which the Victorian proprieties were largely tossed aside for the cult of flaming youth. Following the Volstead Act, speakeasies flourished and the hip-flask became a status symbol. The older generation was scandalized by the latest fads: bobbed hair, short skirts, rolled stocking-tops and "bottle parties."

The national economy was on a wave of prosperity. Land values increased, industry and business expanded, and the stock market reached an all-time high. In Cincinnati a record number of new buildings were under construction. A spacious courthouse was completed and the Dixie Terminal Building, considered the ultimate in architectural design, was erected at the corner of Fourth and Walnut Streets. It featured a vast arcade with a vaulted, ornately decorated ceiling of blue Botticino marble, carved by the finest artisans of the day. The Conservatory mirrored this mounting prosperity in a renewed interest in all branches of music. An affluent society now had time to pursue the fine arts.

Miss Baur had accomplished a great deal in the matter of accreditation. Early in the decade the school was authorized by the Ohio State Department of Education to grant the degrees of Bachelor of Music and Master of Music. In 1923, the Conservatory had become affiliated with the University of Cincinnati's College of Education and, by a reciprocal agreement between the two institutions, full credit was given for certain courses in each school. Conservatory students were permitted to study for degrees at the university whenever the subject studied was applicable to the credentials sought.

During this decade, the summer session became one of the most popular and important features of the Conservatory. With the arrival of the summer students, the school took on a different atmosphere. The entrance hall fairly echoed with shouts of surprise and pleasure as old friends and classmates called greetings; the driveway was crowded with cars from many states. Adding to the confusion were bustling, bewildered parents trying to sort out suitcases and packages from a mountain of luggage. But it was a happy confusion and Miss Baur refused to be annoyed, even when the clamor grew so great we were obliged to close the office door. One morning, upon the arrival of a particular exuberant group, Miss Baur came through the office with her hands to her ears and, in passing, uttered one telling word: "Pandemonium." Yet in spite of the crowded schedule that left her little time for personal matters, she often said the summer school was "nearest her heart."

Under Miss Bertha's direction, the dance curriculum was augmented to include all forms of the dance: ballet, toe, tap, dramatic, and character dancing, as well as the Noyes School of Rhythm and Dalcrose Eurhythmics. After the resignation of Madame Halina Feodorova, the dance department was expertly presided over by Marian LaCour (now Mrs. Fred A. Dowd, of Cincinnati), who brought to the school a wealth of professional experience and her own charming personality. Miss Esther M. Keyes directed the Noyes School of Rhythm and Miss Doris Wulff had charge of the Dalcrose Eurhythmics.

Because Miss Bertha realized what the summer school had meant to Miss Clara and because she herself believed that it fulfilled an urgent need in the music profession, she spared neither effort nor expense to provide the best instruction under the most favorable conditions. She employed the finest instructors available to conduct the master classes, and instituted the short "refresher course," which proved to be a useful innovation for busy teachers. Conservatory students who had attained professional status and were booked for winter concerts also took advantage of the summer school to perfect their programs under the tutelage of master teachers. Aside from the satisfaction of assisting these students in attaining their several goals was the pleasure of reunion with old friends and former students. Miss Baur's door was always open to their visits and she was never too busy to listen to their difficulties or rejoice in their success. One loyal alumna, Mrs. E. H. Hart, who had studied with Miss Clara, set a record for continuous summer attendance. When she was in Cincinnati for the Conservatory's seventieth anniversary celebration, she stated that she had attended forty-two consecutive summer sessions.

At intervals during the summer school, a series of recitals were given by members of the artist faculty to which students had free access. These programs were so well attended that long before the scheduled hour every seat in Concert Hall was taken.

The Dan Beddoe recitals were always eagerly awaited, but his 1931 program was a legendary performance, even for an artist of Mr. Beddoe's stature. It was one of the truly great moments in music. In spite of the ninety-five-degree heat (this was in the days before air conditioning), the hall was filled and dozens of people were standing in the vestibule and outside on the entrance steps. Many students sat on the grass near the open windows so that they could hear the singer even though they were unable to see him. Mr. Beddoe's rendition of Mendelssohn's "The Sorrows of Death" and the stirring aria, "Through the Forests," from Weber's *Der Freischütz* were the highlights of this inspiring program. Among the encores demanded of Mr. Beddoe was the tender ballad "Danny Boy," without which no Beddoe concert was complete. This popular song seemed particularly his and no audience would let him go until it was sung at least once.

Other outstanding faculty members were also heard in recital: Marguerite Mclville Liszniewska, John A. Hoffmann, Karl Kirksmith, Parvin Titus, and Jean ten Have, among others. A feature of the 1925 summer concert series was a recital by Madame Maria Carreras, who came from Rome as a special favor to Miss Baur to conduct a master class in piano.

Since summer school students were obliged to compress so many courses into such a short period, an unusually rigorous schedule was maintained. Time was reserved, however, for picnics, parties, and dances. To relieve the pressure of concentrated study, Miss Baur arranged each week for a special event away from he campus: a trip to Ohio's famous "cave country," a tour of the Kentucky Bluegrass region, or a trip to the Great Serpent Mount at Fort Ancient, Ohio. Visits were also made to educational and cultural landmarks in greater Cincinnati, such as the art museum, Rookwood Pottery, the zoölogical gardens, and the observatory.

The first social event of the season was Miss Baur's annual lawn party, a time for former students to renew old friendships and an opportunity for the newcomers to meet the faculty. It was always a lively occasion. The lawn was lighted with strands of colored lights, and an orchestra furnished appropriate background music. Under the supervision of Mrs. Gabriel, refreshments were served from long tables with centerpieces of fresh flowers from Miss Baur's own garden. White-coated waiters moved among the guests while George Bowman, head waiter, smiling and attentive, made sure everyone was served. Miss Baur was radiantly happy as she welcomed her guests, calling the names of many former students whom she had not seen for two or three years. She had a phenomenal memory for names and seemed never to forget a face.

For many teachers, especially those serving in small communities and rural areas, the summer school was, literally, a "time of refreshment," a period in which to hear the best in music, the opera, and the theatre. Miss Baur urged the students to attend as many programs as possible and, through the generosity of Mrs. Emery and Mrs. Taft, large numbers of tickets were often made available without charge. The Summer Opera Association at the zoölogical gardens had attained a high degree of excellence, presenting such ambitious productions as *Tannhäuser*, *Rigoletto*, *La Forza del Destino*, *Aida*, and *Falstaff*.

The Stuart Walker Company, one of the finest summer stock companies in the country, was in its heyday, playing at the Cox

Theatre in downtown Cincinnati. Feminine theatregoers were swooning over such matinee idols as McKay Morris, Elliott Nugent, Boyd Agin and Eugene Powers. Among the talented actresses who enlivened the scene at the Cox were Spring Byington, Margalo Gilmore, Beulah Bondi, Ilka Chase, and Cincinnati's own Mary Boland. When Mary Boland died in June 1965, Cincinnatians recalled with nostalgia her hilarious performance in *Cradle Snatchers*.[1] In that same cast was Edna Mae Oliver, another Cincinnati favorite, and a young actor destined for a long and illustrious career in show business—Humphrey Bogart.

Perhaps the most anticipated social event of the summer school was the annual boat excursion to Coney Island, Cincinnati's popular amusement park, ten miles up the Ohio River. The trip was made on the *Island Queen*, a stern-wheeler reminiscent of the old-time showboats that plied the river between Pittsburgh and New Orleans in the 1800s. The late afternoon trip was gay, carefree, and lively. On the deck, a calliope piped out river tunes of bygone days, while downstairs in the ballroom an orchestra played for continuous dancing. Those who did not fancy this form of diversion played cards, visited with friends, or relaxed in the deck chairs watching the ever-changing panorama of hills and valleys unfold along the shoreline.

Coney Island offered amusements to suit every age, mood, and whim: the huge ferris wheel spinning its spangle of lights against the backdrop of the Kentucky hills, the roller coaster with its dips and dives, and the loop-the-loop, not recommended for the queasy. The midway was crowded with less strenuous entertainment for the sedate, while the younger set danced in the "Moonlite Jitney Dance Garden." When midnight came and the moon climbed high, the "all aboard" was sounded. The calliope resumed its shrill piping and the merrymakers reluctantly clambered aboard. On this occasion, Miss Baur always waited up to bid us good night and to remind us to observe the "princess pitch" and "fairy footsteps" as we went to our rooms.

As the 1920s came to a close, the summer school enrollment gradually declined. With the increasing number of colleges of music within the framework of the universities and with the convenience of rapid transportation, teachers no longer found it necessary to go beyond the borders of their own states for summer study.

This was the era of the "big-name band." Every student of conducting dreamed of having his own band that would bring him fame and fortune. Miss Baur, always sensitive to cultural currents, was aware of this growing trend and drew heavily upon the personnel of the Cincinnati Symphony Orchestra to meet the demand for teachers in this field: Vladimir Bakaleinikoff, associate conductor, was employed to direct the Conservatory student orchestra; Ary van Leeuwen and Robert Cavally, flutists; Casper Reardon, harpist; Arthur C. Bowen, cellist, and a number of other outstanding orchestra members were added to the instrumental department. Arthur Bowen came to the Cincinnati Symphony as a member of the cello section and was later added to the Conservatory teaching staff. He remains today as a valued member of the College-Conservatory faculty.

About this time a new and novel form of music, having its origin mainly in New Orleans, swept across the country, capturing the imagination of the general public. It was called "Dixieland jazz." Rhythmical, syncopated, almost entirely unwritten, its simple framework and easy tempo lent itself to improvisation. Most professional musicians thought it monotonous, repetitious, and without merit musically. Young people found its rhythm and "jungle beat" exciting. One zealous exponent of this latest craze, a trumpet player from the Deep South, was asked if he wrote his own arrangement. "Man, you don't *write* jazz," he said, "you just *play* it."

There was speculation in music schools as to the effect this new medium would have on music students. Teachers were concerned that it would be used as a shortcut to bypass the serious study of the classics. A controversy arose. Dr. George Leighton felt that jazz had no place within the framework of classical music. Miss Baur disagreed. She maintained that its structure was not altogether without value and that it would eventually find its own niche. She was supported in her opinion by no less an authority than William J. Hall, noted St. Louis organist and composer, who declared at the nationwide observance of Music

Week (1924): "American jazz is a display of musical ingenuity and originality out of which much good may come." In his address to the Conservatory Alumni Assocation, June 5, 1927, Dean David Stanley Smith, director of the department of music at Yale University, had this to say in defense of jazz: "It is pleasant enough recreation and I sometimes enjoy a little of it. . . . It is all right in its place: the dance hall." On the other hand, Dr. Frank Simon, eminent band conductor and founder of the Conservatory band department declared that he would "rather drive a garbage wagon than be a jazz musician. . . . It is only for the feet. There is nothing for the mind and heart."

While musicians discussed the subject, pro and con, Daniel Ericourt, celebrated French pianist-composer and a member of the Conservatory artist faculty, included his own composition, "Pièce en forme de Rag," on a formal recital in the Conservatory concert hall, November 17, 1926. According to one critic, it was the "popular apex" of the program. Said Nina Pugh Smith of the *Cincinnati Times-Star*: "Mr. Ericourt is especially interested in American jazz and believes it is bringing a distinctly new spirit and form to music." Mr. Ericourt first became interested in jazz when he heard it played by Americans in his native France. Speaking of his own composition, he said that it was, of course, of the American school, "since there is no such thing as French jazz."

It is interesting to note that today the College-Conservatory of Music has two jazz ensembles on campus: the Jazz Quintet and the Concert Jazz Band. The latter has been invited to perform at the Fifth International Jazz Festival to be held in Montreux, Switzerland: an honor extended only to the outstanding college and university bands throughout the world.

During the fast, frenetic twenties, Conservatory students, along with the other young people across the nation, danced the Charleston, the Turkey Trot, and the Lindy Hop in Cincinnati's popular night clubs: Castle Farm, Swiss Gardens, and the Hotel Sinton's Chatterbox, where such jazz artists as Duke Ellington, Paul Whiteman, Jan Garber, and Fletcher ("Smack") Henderson brought their orchestras for extended engagements.

The dizzy spiral of this restless, rollicking age kept whirling faster and faster until on October 24, 1929, as the world knows, it came to a jolting stop. On that day the stock market collapsed, leaving thousands of people stunned, incredulous, and penniless. The Depression had begun.

Chapter XXI

RETIREMENT

For age is opportunity no less
Than youth itself, though
in another dress;
And as the evening twilight fades away
The sky is filled with stars invisible by day.
Henry Wadsworth Longfellow, "Morituri Salutamus"

The second semester of 1929-30 opened on a note of gloom. The effects of the Wall Street crash were evident in every phase of the national economy. As the year moved forward, conditions grew worse. Banks failed, fortunes toppled, bread lines became longer, apple vendors appeared on the streets. The country reeled under the impact of the worst depression in its history.

This was perhaps the Conservatory's darkest hour. Every mail brought letters from ambitious young people begging for scholarships, student loans, or work—any kind of work—to defray the cost of tuition. Miss Baur was deeply concerned by the plight of these youthful musicians, frustrated by her inability to do more. She employed every means at her disposal to give assistance, but the Conservatory had no endowment and there were few jobs, even for those with special skills. She herself practiced the strictist economy in personal expenditures, using a large part of her income to help needy students.

As the Depression deepened, appeals for assistance increased. Many students found it necessary to withdraw from school in order to ease the financial burden at home. Music education became a luxury few could afford. Small, privately owned music schools were closing their doors, but Bertha Baur had never been known to acknowledge defeat, and she was determined to take no such drastic action. She enlisted the aid of personal friends, professional men and patrons of the arts, and it was due largely to these loyal friends that the Conservatory

141

was able to remain in operation. Bertha Baur was an inspiration to everyone during these trying times and will long be remembered for her generosity, courage, and compassion.

Then, in July, 1930, came a surprise announcement. Miss Baur informed the public through the medium of the press that she was retiring as director of the Cincinnati Conservatory of Music and, at the same time, offering the school as a gift to the city of Cincinnati through the Institute of Fine Arts. In a letter to the Institute, under date of July 8, 1930, she set forth her reasons. The letter stated in part:

> I have devoted my entire life to building up the institution, and have now reached a time when I desire to see it perpetuated and carried on in the best interests of musical education and development in the City of Cincinnati.
>
> I consider the Cincinnati Institute of Fine Arts the best fitted organization to carry out this purpose, and I desire, therefore, to tender to the Cincinnati Institute of Fine Arts all of the common stock in the Cincinnati Conservatory of Music Company, which owns the institution, and all of the property where it is located.
>
> This will be carrying out the ideal of the founder of the institution, a privilege which I am grateful to be able to help bring about.
>
> This gift of the Conservatory of Music to the City of Cincinnati is the fulfillment of a dream which I have carried with me since my thirty-fifth year; and it is with grateful acknowledgement to those who have made it possible and with very real happiness to myself that I see this active school of music delivered into such permanent and capable hands to function with other activities of our great city.

Three days later, Miss Baur received a letter from Mr. George H. Warrington, vice president of the Institute of Fine Arts, acknowledging her offer and graciously accepting the gift of the Conservatory on behalf of the Institute. The letter read in part:

> In a resolution adopted by the board, I was instructed to inform you that the Institute gratefully accepts the gift of the capital stock of the Cincinnati Conservatory of Music Company which you so generously offer. I was further instructed to express to you the profound appreciation of the importance and generosity of this gift and of the ideals which have prompted it.

The disclosure that the ownership of the Conservatory would now pass to the Institute of Fine Arts was received in Cincinnati with a great deal of surprise and not a little apprehension. The school had been in the Baur family since its founding, and to many of the older residents of the city, any change was unthinkable. Most people greeted Miss Baur's actions as a magnanimous gesture, but this opinion was not unanimous. There were those who intimated that she had devised a clever plan to rid herself of a bankrupt institution under the guise of philanthropy—a master stroke of financial maneuvering. Miss Baur's close friends and associates knew what a great personal sacrifice she had made and were deeply shocked that her motives had been questioned. The truth of the matter is that she had been considering this plan for many years, although it was not generally known. Mrs. Taft had long urged her to take this step, but Bertha Baur had great independence of mind and was reluctant to relinquish control of the school until she could be assured of its permanence. The trustees of the Cincinnati Institute of Fine Arts were among the city's most astute business and professional men, including William Cooper Procter, George Warrington, Robert A. Taft, Herbert G. French, Lucien Wulsin, and Thomas Hogan, Jr. They would undoubtedly have been aware of the Conservatory's liabilities as well as its assets.

Miss Flay Butler, for many years the bursar's assistant, and, consequently, in a position to know the school's financial situation, remarked recently: "While it is true that the Conservatory was in financial difficulties at this time and often ad trouble meeting the payroll, it is equally true that in making this gift, Miss Baur had no thought of evading her contracts, financial or otherwise. Her only concern was for the future of the Conservatory."

"These monetary crises," Miss Butler explained, "were always met with the help of Mrs. Emery, Mrs. Taft, and Mrs. Heine." These three ladies were the preferred stockholders of the Conservatory, which had been incorporated on March 26, 1920, under the corporate name, "Cincinnati Conservatory Company." They were in agreement with Miss Baur that, since she was approaching retirement age, the school should be placed under the management of a foundation and governed by a board of trustees rather than be administered by a single individual.

"The financial difficulties of the Conservatory were not due to mismanagement," Miss Butler went on to say, "but were mainly the result of Miss Baur's unprecedented generosity in providing free tuition for needy students." A revealing instance of Miss Baur's unselfishness and deep concern for the young people of our country is told in a touching little incident. When the board of trustees voted to give her an automobile for her private use, she cried as she protested: "I don't need an automobile. Give me more money for scholarships so that every boy and girl may have his chance for a music education!"[1]

The emotional impact of Miss Baur's decision to relinquish control of the Conservatory cannot be overlooked. In her own words, she had "devoted her entire life to building up the institution," giving herself and her talents to maintaining the educational, artistic, and moral integrity of the school her aunt had crossed an ocean to establish. This gift of her life's work was the crowning proof, if proof were needed, of her generosity and altruism.

According to the terms of acceptance, Miss Baur would continue to live on the Conservatory campus for the duration of her lifetime, making herself available for consultation and advice in the administering of the school. As one of her friends remarked, "She would not only be president emeritus, she would be a sort of 'elder statesman.' "

Bertha Baur could now look back upon more than thirty years of successful school management; an accomplishment which had earned for her an enduring place in the annals of music education. Released from the bondage of daily routine, she was free to travel, to rest, or merely to enjoy the leisure which had been denied her during the busy, crowded years of her leadership. But the bonds of habit are not easily broken, and she was not content to spend her days in aimless inactivity. Unlike many older persons, she did not retreat into a dream world to dwell on past memories (and *what* memories!), but chose to be involved in the mainstream of events.

If Miss Baur had expected to spend her retirement in rest and reflection, she reckoned without the esteem in which she was held by her fellow-citizens. Her opinions were sought on all manner of subjects. Requests came in shoals. She spent long hours in consultation with students, teachers, and administrators. The telephone in President's House rang continuously. Would Miss Baur be kind enough to "pour" at a symphony tea? Could she attend a reception for a visiting dignitary? The requests were varied and seemingly endless.

During this time, Miss Baur was hostess to a number of artists from abroad who happened to be passing through Cincinnati. New regimes had come to power on the continent and, in some instances, had sought to impress their will upon the artistic as well as the political life of the people. Many of these embattled musicians refused to be held captive by the chains of censorship and had come to the United States seeking cultural freedom. Always they found an understanding friend in Bertha Baur, who was a staunch defender of the independence of the creative artist. The great and near-great found their way to the door of the "Grand Old Lady of Music"—columnist Alfred Segal's special designation for Miss Baur—a sobriquet that lasted until the end of her days.

Long after her official retirement, Miss Baur's mail continued to be heavy. She received dozens of letters each week from charities, individuals, and organizations who wished to make use of her name. Composers submitted their compositions for her opinion; music school directors requested her to recommend teachers. An instrumental group trying to raise funds for uniforms begged for a signed photograph or some personal item to be auctioned off at a bazaar; a newly-formed choral society called upon her to suggest a name for their organization. Then there were always former students who quite simply loved her and wished to keep in touch, like the alumna from Tennessee who ended a long and glowing letter by saying: "You are one of the glorious traditions of my life—a legendary personage, like Paderewski in the days of his glory." In the words of a former Conservatory teacher, "Bertha Baur possessed a rare and magnetic personality that inspired the confidence of all those with whom she came in contact."

In the spring of 1937, the Cincinnati Conservatory began preparations for a week-long observance of the seventieth anniversay of its founding. The programs were designed to "commemorate the life of Miss Clara Baur, who had played a leading role in establishing the city's musical prestige, and to honor her successor, Miss Bertha Baur, for her part in bringing the Conservatory to its place of eminence in the music world." Major civic, cultural, and musical organizations of the city cooperated with the Conservatory to make this a memorable occasion. The Honorable Robert A. Taft, United States senator from Ohio and president of the Conservatory Board of Trustees, was general chairman of the week; Mayor Russel Wilson was chairman of "Civic Day," and Dr. John A. Hoffmann had over-all supervision of the various musical programs. In a city-wide proclamation, Mayor Wilson called upon all Cincinnatians to take part in the observance, reminding them of the Conservatory's "notable leadership in the cultural development of the Queen City." A parchment copy of the proclamation was presented to Miss Baur, to be kept in the permanent archives of the school.

Even as the plans for the celebration were being completed, however, it became increasingly evident that Miss Baur would not be able to take an active part in the festivities. Early in February, while crossing Burnet Avenue near the Oak Street entrance to the Conservatory, she was struck by a speeding motorist, sustaining a broken leg and other injuries. This, too, she met with her habitual courage, insisting that she be allowed to come home a few days before the start of the celebration. Only her family and closest friends were permitted to visit her in her sickroom. Propped up in bed on a mountain of pillows, looking regal in a blue velvet bedjacket (the gift of Miss Wanda), she received her callers like a queen granting audience. Among the few visitors permitted to see her was Mrs. E. H. Hart, of Meridian, Mississippi, who recalled that when she came up from the South to "learn music" she rode in a horse-drawn car to the Conservatory, located then at Fourth and Lawrence Streets.

To commemorate "Civic Day," a special concert by the Conservatory Symphony Orchestra, under the baton of Alexander von Kreisler, was broadcast coast to coast over the Columbia Broadcasting network, with Mr. von Kreisler conducting the première of his own composition, *In the Novgorod Forests*. Katherine Baur Lawwill was among the talented young musicians who played that day in the Conservatory Orchestra.

A cantata, *The Song of Songs* by Dr. Carl Hugo Grimm, was also presented by a group of selected voices from the student choruses, with the composer on the podium.

On the program for "Alumni Day," the Cincinnati Mothersingers, directed by Dr. Hoffmann, presented the première of a new choral number, *The Realms of Song*, composed by Mrs. Stanley Lee Clark and Mrs. Louise Harrison Snodgrass. This composition was dedicated to Miss Baur, who had been a patroness of this organization from its beginning.

The Cincinnati Symphony Orchestra was Miss Baur's favorite musical group. She had been an active member of the board of directors for many years, and now, in retirement, she was able to give more time to its promotion. Only a few days before her last and fatal illness, she had scheduled a luncheon for the high school students who were helping with the ticket sales for the Young People's Concerts, and was happily making arrangements to honor these young symphony enthusiasts and their mothers.

Although Miss Baur's firm, elastic steps were beginning to falter and her once-erect posture had become a bit stooped, time had been powerless against the keenness of her mind and the thrust of her youthful spirit. In these last years of her life, she worked enthusiastically for the causes in which she believed, finding personal satisfaction as well as new scope for her many talents. Her sense of humor, her interest in all things musical, and her love for young people remained undiminished.

Always acutely aware of current trends in the field of education, Miss Baur realized that the era of "individualism" was coming to an end. The Cincinnati Conservatory of Music had passed from private ownership, and the closeness and companionship of the small campus had become a casualty of mass education. As the Conservatory was now administered by the Institute of Fine Arts and governed by a board of trustees, its atmosphere had become more and more impersonal. "This invariably happens in an institution when its reputation is built upon the personality of an individual," commented Herbert G. French, prominent Cincinnati attorney. "When the individual dies, the institution as we knew it dies with him."

Bertha Baur did not live to see the Conservatory become a part of the University of Cincinnati. So long as she remained in an advisory capacity, however, she made every effort to maintain the personal touch and to preserve the intimate relationship between student and teacher which she considered essential to the training of young musicians.

Chapter XXII

"LORD, NOW LETTEST THOU THY SERVANT DEPART IN PEACE"

> Because I could not stop for
> Death
> He kindly stopped for me;
> The carriage held but just
> Ourselves
> And Immortality.
>
> Emily Dickinson, "The Chariot"

Bertha Baur had hoped that kind Providence would permit her to witness the Conservatory's "Diamond Jubilee," which would occur in 1942, marking seventy-five years of uninterrupted service to music and musicians. Alas, this last wish was not to be granted. On September 18, 1940, in the early morning hours of that golden autumn day, as the city was beginning to awaken, she received the summons: that inevitable, mysterious summons which mortal man may not refuse to heed. She had devoted her time and effort—in fact, the full measure of her days—to the advancement of music education and to the guidance of the young people who came to the Conservatory for training. She had served long and well. Now her work was finished. Quietly, peacefully, as she slept, she passed from this earthly life into Eternal Light. Gone forever was the warm personality, the gracious smile, and the flash of the clear blue eyes. Her sudden passing had left the city saddened and deprived, but her presence would be very real to those whose lives she had touched. Her strong, adventurous spirit would linger like a benediction as long as the school should last.

When the news of her death was made known, the activities of the Conservatory came to a halt. In the corridors, in the studios, and in the classrooms, students spoke of her in hushed tones. Soon the word sped across the nation by radio, telephone, and telegraph. An avalanche of messages of sympathy and regret poured in from prominent artists and music lovers everywhere, as well as from those who had known her and had been the recipient of her generosity and affection. In his office at the *Cincinnati Post*, Al Segal sat at his desk, stunned and incredulous. Later, he recalled his thoughts: "This is the end of an era. Without Bertha Baur the Conservatory will never be the same. She *was* the Conservatory."

Cincinnatians were shocked at the news of her death. Somehow she had seemed invincible, beyond the long reach of death. There was an outpouring of grief for this beloved citizen whose tireless efforts had added much to the city's musical prestige and artistic attainments. An editorial in the *Cincinnati Times-Star* of September 19 summed up the feelings of Cincinnatians upon learning of their loss. "Generous with her time and talent, Bertha Baur was a guiding spirit in many other cultural enterprises in Cincinnati. Above all else, she was a kindly and gracious gentlewoman whose personal influence left a deep imprint on the life of the city."

Had she regretted the long years of struggle, heartache, and sacrifice? Did she weep for the days of her lost youth, for the happiness and fulfillment that had been denied her? If so, she never betrayed her emotions to family or close friends. In a letter to Mr. George Baur shortly after her death, Miss Annie Howard recalled her last visit with Miss Bertha: "She asked me to read certain passages from the Bible—verses that she loved—and we read together our two favorite passages from the prayer book. Her mind was clear, her face radiant, and I went to my room with a grateful heart that no word of bitterness or disappointment had been uttered." By self-discipline, unremitting toil, and incredible strength of purpose, she had achieved the two-pronged goal toward which Miss Clara had directed her efforts: to bring the Conservatory into world-wide recognition and to provide for its perpetuation. She had lived to see this dream come to fruition, a boon that is granted to only a few.

Bertha Baur's complex nature and diverse talents may be traced to her ancestry: the keen, analytical mind of the German scholar; the courage and fortitude of the embattled clergymen who risked exile, torture, and death to insure freedom of worship; the imperiousness of a proud old family; the poise and confidence of the Bavarian nobility, and the quiet dignity of the Saxon farmer who found satisfaction and contentment in the cultivation of his land. If, however, one dominant trait could be ascribed to Bertha Baur, that trait would be generosity. Like the principal theme of an orchestral score, recurring in many rhythms and in different patterns, generosity wove itself into the composition of her daily life. As the *Cincinnati Enquirer* so aptly observed, "She was a friend of all the world in artistic need."

As the thread of life grew shorter, Miss Baur's family and friends noted a subtle change. She seemed more thoughtful, more introspective, less assertive. The passing of so many of her old friends and contemporaries—Mrs. Taft, Mrs. Emery, Tirindelli, Ysaÿe, and Theodor Bohlmann (the latter two had died in the same year)—had made a deep impression upon her. Yet she did not speak of death. Her days were too full to dwell upon such a remote possibility. She spoke confidently of the future: the Conservatory's role in the changing values of the music world, the gifted young artists whose careers she was helping to fashion, and the high school students whose lives she was guiding into a deeper appreciation of classical music.

Mrs. Lawwill recalls that Miss Baur had not been well during the summer preceding her death but had seemed to make a full recovery. She was in good spirits and was looking forward with enthusiasm to another school year. On Monday evening, September 16, she had been to dinner with the George Crabbs family, but had returned home to retire early. Sometime during the night she was awakened by severe cramps in her arms and hands. When they grew worse, she was taken to Holmes Hospital, where she died less than forty-eight hours later. She was in the eighty-second year of her life, sixty-four of which she had given unstintingly to the Cincinnati Conservatory of music.

For her last earthly journey, she was dressed in the robe and hood of her honorary degree from the University of Cincinnati, of which she had been justly proud. Loving hands placed her in the casket which was carried to the flower-laden music room in South Hall. Here she reposed while hundreds of grieving friends came to pay their last respects to the "Grand Old Lady of Music." Two services preceded the burial in Spring Grove

151

Cemetery, the first being conducted privately in South Hall for the Conservatory personnel. The second one was held in Christ Church, where she had been a communicant for many years. Mrs. Lawwill remembers that it was a beautiful autumn day, warm and cloudless. "I sat on the veranda of South Hall," she said, "while the private service was in progress, waiting to join the funeral procession to Christ Church."

The church was filled to overflowing and those who were unable to be seated inside stood silently in the vestibule or outside on the steps. Fourth Street, where Christ Church is located, was closed to traffic for the duration of the service. Dr. Parvin Titus, organist and choirmaster and teacher of organ at the Conservatory, was in charge of the music. Special numbers were played by a string quartet composed of Conservatory faculty members: Howard Colf, first violin; Julian de Pulikowski, second violin; Mikail Stolarevsky, viola, and Arthur C. Bowen, violoncello. These four men, selected for this occasion, were also members of the Cincinnati Symphony Orchestra, the organization to which Miss Baur had given so much of her time and energy. Among the musical numbers chosen were Handel's *Largo*, Mozart's *Ave Verum*, and excerpts from the works of Beethoven, Haydn, and Cesar Franck.

There was silence in the sanctuary except for an occasional scarcely audible whisper and the sound of moving feet as the mourners knelt on the prayer rails. Dr. Nelson Burroughs, Miss Baur's dear friend and beloved rector, spoke with deep emotion: "Lord, now lettest Thou Thy servant depart in peace, according to Thy word." Now it was over. An era had come to a close and the career of this remarkable woman had passed into history. Alice Baur Hodges said it well: "Cousin Bertha's permanent memorial is not so much in the school she helped to build as in the lives of those who have gone out from the Conservatory with her blessing, with the remembrance of her inspiring personality."

CHAPTER NOTES

Chapter I

1. These exquisite carvings were fashioned by a Cincinnati woodcarver, Henry L. Fry, son of the famous sculptor William Fry, whose ornamental engravings have adorned so many churches, schools, and other public buildings in Cincinnati.
2. This window was the gift of the faculty and alumni in memory of Miss Clara Baur.

Chapter II

1. Miss Clara Baur's Last Will and Testament is on file in the Hamilton County Courthouse, Cincinnati, Ohio.
2. From records in the possession of Mrs. J. Kenton Lawwill (Katherine Baur), daughter of George A. Baur; from Mrs. Virginia (Baur) Brown, of Sunland, California, and *Who's Who in America*, 1928-29, Vol. 15.
3. *Genealogie der Familie Baur*, compiled and written by Theodor Baur, Sr., of Cincinnati, Ohio. Undated. In the possession of Mrs. Virginia Brown, Sunland, California.

Chapter III

1. The history of the Baur family was obtained from the *Genealogie der Familie Baur*, compiled and written by Theodor Baur, Sr., and from a more recent history written by Mrs. Virginia (Baur) Brown, of Sunland, California. Completed by Mrs. Brown in 1968 and in her possession.
2. From *The American Journal of Archaeology*, Vol. 56, No. 1, January 1952, Stephen B. Luce, Editor, Necrology.
3. Bertrand Baur was the first son of the Reverend and Mrs. Emil Gottlieb Ludwig Baur, born April 13, 1860, in Pittsburgh, Pennsylvania.
4. From the Herzer family genealogy, supplied by Mrs. Herman A. Herzer, of Lakewood, Ohio.
5. Mrs. Kockritz, well-known pianist and accompanist, is presently on the faculty of the College-Conservatory of Music of the University of Cincinnati. She is the daughter of Cornelia (Herzer) and John Christian Otto, and the wife of Hubert Kockritz, also a member of the College-Conservatory of Music teaching staff.

153

6. From a letter to the author from Herman Herzer's son, August Scheffel Herzer, of Zanesville, Ohio, dated June 12, 1967.

7. William R. Coates, *A History of Cuyahoga County and the City of Cleveland*, 3 vols. (Chicago: The American Historical Society, 1924), 1:6.

8. Information received from Mrs. Robert Fawcett, Lakewood, Ohio, great-granddaughter of Dr. Herzer.

Chapter IV

1. From the manuscript *Ora Labora*, by Mrs. Lela Puffer, of Flint, Michigan. Used by permission of the author.

2. This document is in the possession of the University of Michigan Historical Collections.

3. A short history of the Colony, written by one of the colonists, undated and unsigned, states that the colony was "settled in December 1862, Section 29, Town 17, N.R. 10 East from the sand ridge down to Wild Fowl Bay where town lots were laid out and buildings were erected." In the University of Michigan Historical Collections.

Further proof that the Colony was settled in 1862 is contained in a letter dated December, 1862, to Governor Austin Blair from John F. Driggs, introducing Emil Baur to the governor. In the letter, Mr. Driggs explains that Emil Baur had recently organized the colony of Ora Labora. In the University of Michigan Historical Collections.

4. Ibid.

5. From *Ora Labora*, by Mrs. Lela Puffer. Quoted by permission of the author.

6. The background for this period in the Colony's existence was found in newspaper clippings from the Bay City *Times* and the Detroit *News*. In the University of Michigan Historical Collections.

7. Henry David Thoreau, *Walden and Other Writings*, ed. Brooks Atkinson (New York: Modern Library, 1937).

Chapter V

1. From an advertisement in the *Ann Arbor Courier* in the possession of Mrs. Robert Morse. It is undated.

2. Emil Baur was a frequent contributor to *Der Christliche Apologete*, published and edited in Cincinnati by Reverend Albert Nast.

3. Mrs. Morse states that, according to her father's recollections, after the Colony was well established and the buildings completed, the Baur family maintained a permanent residence in Ann Arbor. They occupied their cottage at *Ora Labora* only in the seasons of planting and harvesting and at certain other times when Emil Baur's presence was required in administrative duties.

4. Mrs. Hodges, the daughter of Nann (Hill) and Emil Baur, son of Theodor Baur, Jr., is a cousin of Miss Bertha Baur.

Chapter VI

1. The March, 1913 issue of *Sharps and Flats* was dedicated to the memory of Miss Clara Baur.
2. Lewis A. Leonard, *Greater Cincinnati and Its People*, 4 vols. (New York: Lewis Historical Publishing Company, Inc., 1927), vol. 4. pg. 547.

Chapter VII

1. *New York Musical Courier*, June 21, 1917, Vol. LXXIV, No. 13. Whole No. 1932.
2. The author is indebted to Mrs. Alice Hodges for this amusing incident.

Chapter VIII

1. *Musical Courier*, November 3, 1916, Vol. LXXIII, No. 18, pg. 7.

Chapter IX

1. Charles Frederic Goss, *Cincinnati: The Queen City* (Cincinnati: S. J. Clark Publishing Co., 1912), 1:377.
2. Ibid.
3. George Mortimer Roe, *Cincinnati: The Queen City of the West* (Cincinnati: Times-Star Company, 1895), 1:223.
4. Lewis A. Leonard, *Greater Cincinnati and Its People*, 4 vols. (New York: Lewis Historical Publishing Company, Inc., 1927), 4:544.
5. Goss, op. cit.
6. *The American Guide Series*, Ohio Writers' Project (Cincinnati: Weisen-Hart Press, 1788).
7. Ibid.

Chapter X

1. Charles Frederic Goss, *Cincinnati: The Queen City* (Cincinnati: S. J. Clarke Publishing Co., 1912), 1:377.
2. This catalog is in the possession of the Cincinnati Historical Society.
3. Ibid.
4. This is the only one of the Conservatory's five locations extant today. It is occupied by Becker Brothers, clothiers.
5. Lewis A. Leonard, *Greater Cincinnati and Its People*, 4 vols. (New York: Lewis Historical Publishing Company, Inc., 1927), 1:329.
6. Ibid.

7. George Mortimer Roe, *Cincinnati: The Queen City of the West* (Cincinnati: Times-Star Company, 1895), 1:223.

8. Not to be confused with Bertha Baur's niece, Wanda Constance Baur, daughter of Bertrand Baur.

Chapter XI

1. The background for this period in Cincinnati's history is taken from the *American Guide Series*, Ohio Writers' Project (Cincinnati: Weisen-Hart Press, 1788). Used by permission of the City of Cincinnati Council, Aug. 6, 1971.

2. The author is indebted to Mrs. Alice Hodges for this incident.

3. From the March, 1913 issue of *Sharps and Flats*.

Chapter XII

1. *New York Musical Courier*, March 29, 1917, Vol. LXXIV, No. 13, Whole No. 1931.

Chapter XVIII

1. Also honored at this time were: Randall J. Condon, Superintendent of Cincinnati Public Schools, Doctor of Laws; Arthur Lowenstein, Doctor of Science; George Frederic Dick and his wife Gladys Dick, Doctors of Science.

Chapter XIX

1. A source of background information for this period in Pier Tirindelli's life was found in *Mrs. Jack*, by Louise Hall Tharp, Little, Brown & Company, Boston, 1965. (Author's permission)

2. Published by Oliver, Ditson Company, Boston, in 1925.

Chapter XX

1. A Comedy in three acts, by Russel Medcraft and Norma Mitchell, published by Samuel French, Inc., New York.

Chapter XXI

1. Lewis A. Leonard, *Greater Cincinnati and Its People*, 4 vols. (New York: Lewis Historical Publishing Company, Inc., 1927), 4:459.